ALL GLORY TO ŚRĪ GURU AND GAURĀṄGA

ŚRĪMAD BHĀGAVATAM

of

KṚṢṆA-DVAIPĀYANA VYĀSA

सतामयं सारभृतां निसर्गो
यदर्थवाणीश्रुतिचेतसामपि ।
प्रतिक्षणं नव्यवदच्युतस्य यत्
स्त्रिया विटानामिव साधुवार्ता ॥ २ ॥

satām ayaṁ sāra-bhṛtāṁ nisargo
yad-artha-vāṇī-śruti-cetasām api
prati-kṣaṇaṁ navya-vad acyutasya yat
striyā viṭānām iva sādhu vārtā (p. 3)

BOOKS by
His Divine Grace
A. C. Bhaktivedanta Swami Prabhupāda

Bhagavad-gītā As It Is
Śrīmad-Bhāgavatam, Cantos 1–10 (30 vols.)
Śrī Caitanya-caritāmṛta (17 vols.)
Teachings of Lord Caitanya
The Nectar of Devotion
The Nectar of Instruction
Śrī Īśopaniṣad
Easy Journey to Other Planets
Kṛṣṇa Consciousness: The Topmost Yoga System
Kṛṣṇa, the Supreme Personality of Godhead (3 vols.)
Perfect Questions, Perfect Answers
Dialectical Spiritualism—A Vedic View of Western Philosophy
Teachings of Lord Kapila, the Son of Devahūti
Transcendental Teachings of Prahlād Mahārāja
Teachings of Queen Kuntī
Kṛṣṇa, the Reservoir of Pleasure
The Science of Self-Realization
The Path of Perfection
Life Comes From Life
The Perfection of Yoga
Beyond Birth and Death
On the Way to Kṛṣṇa
Geetār-gan (Bengali)
Vairāgya-vidyā (Bengali)
Buddhi-yoga (Bengali)
Bhakti-ratna-bolī (Bengali)
Rāja-vidyā: The King of Knowledge
Elevation to Kṛṣṇa Consciousness
Kṛṣṇa Consciousness: The Matchless Gift
Back to Godhead magazine (founder)

A complete catalog is available upon request.

Bhaktivedanta Book Trust
3764 Watseka Avenue
Los Angeles, California 90034

ŚRĪMAD BHĀGAVATAM

Tenth Canto

"The Summum Bonum"

(Special Edition—Chapter 13)

With the Original Sanskrit Text, Its Roman Transliteration, Synonyms, Translation and Elaborate Purports

by

His Divine Grace
A.C. Bhaktivedanta Swami Prabhupāda
Founder-*Ācārya* of the International Society for Krishna Consciousness

THE BHAKTIVEDANTA BOOK TRUST
Los Angeles · New York · London · Paris · Frankfurt · Bombay

Readers interested in the subject matter of this book are invited by the International Society for Krishna Consciousness to visit any ISKCON center worldwide (see address list in back of book) or to correspond with the Secretary:

International Society for Krishna Consciousness
3764 Watseka Avenue
Los Angeles, California 90034

First Printing, 1980: 20,000 copies

Printed in the United States of America

Library of Congress Cataloging in Publication Data (Revised)

Puranas. Bhāgavatapurāna.
Śrīmad-Bhāgavatam.

Includes bibliographical references and indexes.
CONTENTS: Canto 1. Creation. 3 v.—Canto 2. The cosmic manifestation. 2 v.—Canto 3. The status quo. 4 v.—Canto 4. The creation of the Fourth Order. 4 v.—Canto 5. The creative impetus. 2 v.
1. Chaitanya, 1486-1534. I. Bhaktivedanta Swami, A. C., 1896-1977 II. Title.
BL1135.P7A22 1972 73-169353
ISBN 0-89213-107-1

Table of Contents

Foreword *vii*
Preface *ix*
Introduction *xiii*

CHAPTER THIRTEEN
The Stealing of the Boys and Calves by Brahmā 1
Chapter Summary 1
The Lord's Activities Are Very Confidential 5
Kṛṣṇa Is Always Visible to His Devotees 9
The Devotee of the Lord Is Free from Fear 13
Brahmā Steals the Calves and Boys 16
Kṛṣṇa Expands as the Calves and Boys to Astonish Brahmā 19
The Supreme Lord Is Everything 29
Baladeva Surprised by Kṛṣṇa's *Yogamāyā* 35
Brahmā Bewildered by His Own Mystic Power 46
The Glance of Viṣṇu Creates the Devotees' Desires 53
All Living Entities Are Servants of Kṛṣṇa 55
The Supreme Lord Known Only by Devotion 61
Brahmā Stunned by Transcendental Bliss 64
The Lord Is One Without a Second 73

Appendixes 79
The Author 80
References 83
Glossary 85
Sanskrit Pronunciation Guide 89
Index of Sanskrit Verses 93
General Index 97

Foreword

This is the final *Śrīmad-Bhāgavatam* volume translated by His Divine Grace A. C. Bhaktivedanta Swami Prabhupāda, the founder-*ācārya* of the International Society for Krishna Consciousness. It is smaller than the earlier volumes because it ends where the renowned author stopped translating just before his departure from this mortal world on November 14, 1977, at the Kṛṣṇa-Balarāma Mandira in Vṛndāvana, India.

The first part of this volume was produced in the usual fashion. Śrīla Prabhupāda would sit and read silently from the Sanskrit text and then speak the translation and commentary into his dictaphone. Later, due to illness, it became necessary for his disciples to assist him personally.

In these last days Śrīla Prabhupāda was gravely ill. Unable to eat for weeks, his health had deteriorated, making even the slightest movement excruciatingly painful.

As he lay still, a devotee would softly read the Sanskrit to him. Another disciple, sitting on his bed, held the microphone to him, nearly touching his mouth. And then Śrīla Prabhupāda would speak, voice sometimes barely audible.

These recordings, made in his quarters at the temple, constitute the balance of this book.

In these final moments, the physician attending His Divine Grace confided that an ordinary man in such critical condition would have been crying out from the intense pain. Śrīla Prabhupāda's disciples were awestruck as they watched their spiritual master work quietly, undisturbed.

In the last part of the book we find Śrīla Prabhupāda's usual clarity of thought, constant scriptural references, scrupulous attention to detail, and rigorous philosophical exposition fully intact, just as they were in the preceding twenty-nine volumes of the *Śrīmad-Bhāgavatam.*

Śrīla Prabhupāda's last days and this translation will stand as an inspiring reminder that even the severest material circumstances cannot impede the activities of a pure devotee of the Supreme Personality of Godhead.

—The Publishers

Preface

We must know the present need of human society. And what is that need? Human society is no longer bounded by geographical limits to particular countries or communities. Human society is broader than in the Middle Ages, and the world tendency is toward one state or one human society. The ideals of spiritual communism, according to *Śrīmad-Bhāgavatam*, are based more or less on the oneness of the entire human society, nay, of the entire energy of living beings. The need is felt by great thinkers to make this a successful ideology. *Śrīmad-Bhāgavatam* will fill this need in human society. It begins, therefore, with the aphorism of Vedānta philosophy *janmādy asya yataḥ* to establish the ideal of a common cause.

Human society, at the present moment, is not in the darkness of oblivion. It has made rapid progress in the field of material comforts, education and economic development throughout the entire world. But there is a pinprick somewhere in the social body at large, and therefore there are large-scale quarrels, even over less important issues. There is need of a clue as to how humanity can become one in peace, friendship and prosperity with a common cause. *Śrīmad-Bhāgavatam* will fill this need, for it is a cultural presentation for the respiritualization of the entire human society.

Śrīmad-Bhāgavatam should be introduced also in the schools and colleges, for it is recommended by the great student-devotee Prahlāda Mahārāja in order to change the demoniac face of society.

kaumāra ācaret prājño
dharmān bhāgavatān iha
durlabhaṁ mānuṣaṁ janma
tad apy adhruvam arthadam
(*Bhāg.* 7.6.1)

Disparity in human society is due to lack of principles in a godless civilization. There is God, or the Almighty One, from whom everything emanates, by whom everything is maintained and in whom everything is merged to rest. Material science has tried to find the ultimate source of creation very insufficiently, but it is a fact that there is one ultimate source of everything that be. This ultimate source is explained rationally and authoritatively in the beautiful *Bhāgavatam*, or *Śrīmad-Bhāgavatam*.

Śrīmad-Bhāgavatam is the transcendental science not only for knowing the ultimate source of everything but also for knowing our relation with Him and our duty toward perfection of the human society on the basis of this perfect knowledge. It is powerful reading matter in the Sanskrit language, and it is now rendered into English elaborately so that simply by a careful reading one will know God perfectly well, so much so that the reader will be sufficiently educated to defend himself from the onslaught of atheists. Over and above this, the reader will be able to convert others to accepting God as a concrete principle.

Śrīmad-Bhāgavatam begins with the definition of the ultimate source. It is a bona fide commentary on the *Vedānta-sūtra* by the same author, Śrīla Vyāsadeva, and gradually it develops into nine cantos up to the highest state of God realization. The only qualification one needs to study this great book of transcendental knowledge is to proceed step by step cautiously and not jump forward haphazardly like with an ordinary book. It should be gone through chapter by chapter, one after another. The reading matter is so arranged with its original Sanskrit text, its English transliteration, synonyms, translation and purports so that one is sure to become a God-realized soul at the end of finishing the first nine cantos.

The Tenth Canto is distinct from the first nine cantos because it deals directly with the transcendental activities of the Personality of Godhead Śrī Kṛṣṇa. One will be unable to capture the effects of the Tenth Canto without going through the first nine cantos. The book is complete in twelve cantos, each independent, but it is good for all to read them in small installments one after another.

I must admit my frailties in presenting *Śrīmad-Bhāgavatam*, but still I am hopeful of its good reception by the thinkers and leaders of society on the strength of the following statement of *Śrīmad-Bhāgavatam* (1.5.11):

tad-vāg-visargo janatāgha-viplavo
yasmin prati-ślokam abaddhavaty api

nāmāny anantasya yaśo 'ṅkitāni yac
chṛṇvanti gāyanti gṛṇanti sādhavaḥ

"On the other hand, that literature which is full with descriptions of the transcendental glories of the name, fame, form and pastimes of the unlimited Supreme Lord is a transcendental creation meant to bring about a revolution in the impious life of a misdirected civilization. Such transcendental literatures, even though irregularly composed, are heard, sung and accepted by purified men who are thoroughly honest."

Oṁ tat sat

A. C. Bhaktivedanta Swami

Introduction

"This *Bhāgavata Purāṇa* is as brilliant as the sun, and it has arisen just after the departure of Lord Kṛṣṇa to His own abode, accompanied by religion, knowledge, etc. Persons who have lost their vision due to the dense darkness of ignorance in the age of Kali shall get light from this *Purāṇa*." (*Śrīmad-Bhāgavatam* 1.3.43)

The timeless wisdom of India is expressed in the *Vedas*, ancient Sanskrit texts that touch upon all fields of human knowledge. Originally preserved through oral tradition, the *Vedas* were first put into writing five thousand years ago by Śrīla Vyāsadeva, the "literary incarnation of God." After compiling the *Vedas*, Vyāsadeva set forth their essence in the aphorisms known as *Vedānta-sūtras*. *Śrīmad-Bhāgavatam* is Vyāsadeva's commentary on his own *Vedānta-sūtras*. It was written in the maturity of his spiritual life under the direction of Nārada Muni, his spiritual master. Referred to as "the ripened fruit of the tree of Vedic literature," *Śrīmad-Bhāgavatam* is the most complete and authoritative exposition of Vedic knowledge.

After compiling the *Bhāgavatam*, Vyāsa impressed the synopsis of it upon his son, the sage Śukadeva Gosvāmī. Śukadeva Gosvāmī subsequently recited the entire *Bhāgavatam* to Mahārāja Parīkṣit in an assembly of learned saints on the bank of the Ganges at Hastināpura (now Delhi). Mahārāja Parīkṣit was the emperor of the world and was a great *rājarṣi* (saintly king). Having received a warning that he would die within a week, he renounced his entire kingdom and retired to the bank of the Ganges to fast until death and receive spiritual enlightenment. The *Bhāgavatam* begins with Emperor Parīkṣit's sober inquiry to Śukadeva Gosvāmī: "You are the spiritual master of great saints and devotees. I am therefore begging you to show the way of perfection for all persons, and especially for one who is about to die. Please let me know what a man should hear, chant, remember and worship, and also what he should not do. Please explain all this to me."

Śukadeva Gosvāmī's answer to this question, and numerous other questions posed by Mahārāja Parīkṣit, concerning everything from the nature of the self to the origin of the universe, held the assembled sages in rapt attention continuously for the seven days leading to the King's death. The sage Sūta Gosvāmī, who was present on the bank of the Ganges when Śukadeva Gosvāmī first recited *Śrīmad-Bhāgavatam*, later repeated the *Bhāgavatam* before a gathering of sages in the forest of Naimiṣāraṇya. Those sages, concerned about the spiritual welfare of the people in general, had gathered to perform a long, continuous chain of sacrifices to counteract the degrading influence of the incipient age of Kali. In response to the sages' request that he speak the essence of Vedic wisdom, Sūta Gosvāmī repeated from memory the entire eighteen thousand verses of *Śrīmad-Bhāgavatam*, as spoken by Śukadeva Gosvāmī to Mahārāja Parīkṣit.

The reader of *Śrīmad-Bhāgavatam* hears Sūta Gosvāmī relate the questions of Mahārāja Parīkṣit and the answers of Śukadeva Gosvāmī. Also, Sūta Gosvāmī sometimes responds directly to questions put by Śaunaka Ṛṣi, the spokesman for the sages gathered at Naimiṣāraṇya. One therefore simultaneously hears two dialogues: one between Mahārāja Parīkṣit and Śukadeva Gosvāmī on the bank of the Ganges, and another at Naimiṣāraṇya between Sūta Gosvāmī and the sages at Naimiṣāraṇya Forest, headed by Śaunaka Ṛṣi. Furthermore, while instructing King Parīkṣit, Śukadeva Gosvāmī often relates historical episodes and gives accounts of lengthy philosophical discussions between such great souls as the saint Maitreya and his disciple Vidura. With this understanding of the history of the *Bhāgavatam*, the reader will easily be able to follow its intermingling of dialogues and events from various sources. Since philosophical wisdom, not chronological order, is most important in the text, one need only be attentive to the subject matter of *Śrīmad-Bhāgavatam* to appreciate fully its profound message.

The translator of this edition compares the *Bhāgavatam* to sugar candy—wherever you taste it, you will find it equally sweet and relishable. Therefore, to taste the sweetness of the *Bhāgavatam*, one may begin by reading any of its volumes. After such an introductory taste, however, the serious reader is best advised to go back to Volume One of the First Canto and then proceed through the *Bhāgavatam*, volume after volume, in its natural order.

This edition of the *Bhāgavatam* is the first complete English translation of this important text with an elaborate commentary, and it is the first widely available to the English-speaking public. It is the product of the scholarly and devotional effort of His Divine Grace A. C. Bhaktivedanta Swami Prabhupāda, the world's most distinguished teacher of Indian religious and philosophical thought. His consummate Sanskrit scholarship and intimate familiarity with Vedic culture and thought as well as the modern way of life combine to reveal to the West a magnificent exposition of this important classic.

Readers will find this work of value for many reasons. For those interested in the classical roots of Indian civilization, it serves as a vast reservoir of detailed information on virtually every one of its aspects. For students of comparative philosophy and religion, the *Bhāgavatam* offers a penetrating view into the meaning of India's profound spiritual heritage. To sociologists and anthropologists, the *Bhāgavatam* reveals the practical workings of a peaceful and scientifically organized Vedic culture, whose institutions were integrated on the basis of a highly developed spiritual world-view. Students of literature will discover the *Bhāgavatam* to be a masterpiece of majestic poetry. For students of psychology, the text provides important perspectives on the nature of consciousness, human behavior and the philosophical study of identity. Finally, to those seeking spiritual insight, the *Bhāgavatam* offers simple and practical guidance for attainment of the highest self-knowledge and realization of the Absolute Truth. The entire multivolume text, presented by the Bhaktivedanta Book Trust, promises to occupy a significant place in the intellectual, cultural and spiritual life of modern man for a long time to come.

—The Publishers

His Divine Grace
A. C. Bhaktivedanta Swami Prabhupāda
Founder-Ācārya of the International Society for Krishna Consciousness

Śrīla Prabhupāda's room in the Kṛṣṇa-Balarāma Mandira, where he spent his final days translating this volume of the *Śrīmad-Bhāgavatam.*

The Kṛṣṇa-Balarāma Mandira in Vṛndāvana, India.

PLATE ONE

After selecting a pleasing location on the riverbank, Lord Kṛṣṇa and His friends opened their baskets of food and began eating in great transcendental pleasure. Like the whorl of a lotus flower surrounded by its petals and leaves, Kṛṣṇa sat in the center, encircled by lines of His friends, who all looked very beautiful. Every one of them was trying to look forward toward Kṛṣṇa, thinking that Kṛṣṇa might look toward him. Among the cowherd boys, some placed their lunch on flowers, some on leaves, fruits, or bunches of leaves, some actually in their baskets, some on the bark of trees and some on rocks. This is what the children imagined to be their plates as they ate their lunch. All the cowherd boys enjoyed their lunch with Kṛṣṇa, showing one another the different tastes of the different varieties of preparations they had brought from home. Tasting one another's preparations, they began to laugh and make one another laugh. In this way they all enjoyed their lunch in the forest. (*pp. 6–10*)

PLATE TWO

One day, five or six nights before the completion of the year, Kṛṣṇa, tending the calves, entered the forest along with Balarāma. Thereafter, while pasturing atop Govardhana Hill, the cows looked down to find some green grass and saw their calves pasturing near Vṛndāvana, not very far away. When the cows saw their own calves from the top of Govardhana Hill, they forgot themselves and their caretakers because of increased affection, and although the path was very rough, they ran toward their calves with great anxiety, each running as if with one pair of legs. Their milk bags full and flowing with milk, their heads and tails raised, and their humps moving with their necks, they ran forcefully until they reached their calves to feed them. The cowherd men, having been unable to check the cows from going to their calves, felt simultaneously ashamed and angry. They crossed the rough road with great difficulty, but when they came down and saw their own sons, they were overwhelmed by great affection. At that time, all the thoughts of the cowherd men merged in the mellow of paternal love, which was aroused by the sight of their sons. Experiencing a great attraction, their anger completely disappearing, they lifted their sons, embraced them in their arms and enjoyed the highest pleasure by smelling their sons' heads. (*pp. 29–33*)

PLATE THREE

While Lord Brahmā looked on, all the calves and the boys tending them immediately appeared to have complexions the color of bluish rainclouds and to be dressed in yellow silken garments. All those personalities had four arms, holding conchshell, disc, mace and lotus flower in Their hands. They wore helmets on Their heads, earrings on Their ears and garlands of forest flowers around Their necks. On the upper portion of the right side of Their chests was the emblem of the goddess of fortune. Furthermore, They wore armlets on Their arms, the Kaustubha gem around Their necks, which were marked with three lines like a conchshell, and bracelets on Their wrists. With bangles on Their ankles, ornaments on Their feet, and sacred belts around Their waists, They all appeared very beautiful. Those Viṣṇu forms, by Their pure smiling, which resembled the increasing light of the moon, and by the sidelong glances of Their reddish eyes, created and protected the desires of Their own devotees, as if by the modes of passion and goodness. Thus Lord Brahmā saw the Supreme Brahman, by whose energy this entire universe, with its moving and nonmoving living beings, is manifested. He also saw at the same time all the calves and boys as the Lord's expansions. (*pp. 49–63*)

PLATE FOUR

Lord Brahmā saw the Absolute Truth—who is one without a second, who possesses full knowledge and who is unlimited—assuming the role of a child in a family of cowherd men and standing all alone, just as before, with a morsel of food in His hand, searching everywhere for the calves and His cowherd friends. After seeing this, Lord Brahmā hastily got down from his swan carrier, fell down like a golden rod and touched the lotus feet of Lord Kṛṣṇa with the tips of the four crowns on his heads. Offering his obeisances, he bathed the feet of Kṛṣṇa with the water of his tears of joy. Rising and falling again and again at the lotus feet of Lord Kṛṣṇa for a long time, Lord Brahmā remembered over and over the Lord's greatness he had just seen. Then, rising very gradually and wiping his two eyes, Lord Brahmā looked up at Mukunda. Lord Brahmā, his head bent low, his mind concentrated and his body trembling, very humbly began, with faltering words, to offer praise to Lord Kṛṣṇa. (*pp. 73–78*)

Brahma-kuṇḍa, the site where Lord Brahmā offered his prayers to Lord Kṛṣṇa after the pastime known as *Brahma-vimohana-līlā*.

CHAPTER THIRTEEN

The Stealing of the Boys and Calves by Brahmā

This chapter describes Lord Brahmā's attempt to take away the calves and cowherd boys, and it also describes the bewilderment of Lord Brahmā and finally the clearance of his illusion.

Although the incident concerning Aghāsura had been performed one year before, when the cowherd boys were five years old, when they were six years old they said, "It happened today." What happened was this. After killing Aghāsura, Kṛṣṇa, along with His associates the cowherd boys, went for a picnic within the forest. The calves, being allured by green grasses, gradually went far away, and therefore Kṛṣṇa's associates became a little agitated and wanted to bring back the calves. Kṛṣṇa, however, encouraged the boys by saying, "You take your tiffin without being agitated. I shall go find the calves." And thus the Lord departed. Then, just to examine the potency of Kṛṣṇa, Lord Brahmā took away all the calves and cowherd boys and kept them in a secluded place.

When Kṛṣṇa was unable to find the calves and boys, He could understand that this was a trick performed by Brahmā. Then the Supreme Personality of Godhead, the cause of all causes, in order to please Lord Brahmā, as well as His own associates and their mothers, expanded Himself to become the calves and boys, exactly as they were before. In this way, He discovered another pastime. A special feature of this pastime was that the mothers of the cowherd boys thus became more attached to their respective sons, and the cows became more attached to their calves. After nearly a year, Baladeva observed that all the cowherd boys and calves were expansions of Kṛṣṇa. Thus He inquired from Kṛṣṇa and was informed of what had happened.

When one full year had passed, Brahmā returned and saw that Kṛṣṇa was still engaged as usual with His friends and the calves and cows. Then Kṛṣṇa exhibited all the calves and cowherd boys as four-armed forms of Nārāyaṇa. Brahmā could then understand Kṛṣṇa's potency, and he was astonished by the pastimes of Kṛṣṇa, his worshipable Lord. Kṛṣṇa, however, bestowed His causeless mercy upon Brahmā and released him from illusion. Thus Brahmā began to offer prayers to glorify the Supreme Personality of Godhead.

TEXT 1

श्रीशुक उवाच

साधु पृष्टं महाभाग त्वया भागवतोत्तम ।
यन्नूतनयसीशस्य शृण्वन्नपि कथां मुहुः ॥ १ ॥

śrī-śuka uvāca
sādhu pṛṣṭaṁ mahā-bhāga
tvayā bhāgavatottama
yan nūtanayasīśasya
śṛṇvann api kathāṁ muhuḥ

śrī-śukaḥ uvāca—Śukadeva Gosvāmī said; *sādhu pṛṣṭam*—I have been very much honored by your inquiry; *mahā-bhāga*—you are a greatly fortunate personality; *tvayā*—by you; *bhāgavata-uttama*—O best of devotees; *yat*—because; *nūtanayasi*—you are making newer and newer; *īśasya*—of the Supreme Personality of Godhead; *śṛṇvan api*—although you are continuously hearing; *kathām*—the pastimes; *muhuḥ*—again and again.

TRANSLATION

Śrīla Śukadeva Gosvāmī said: O best of devotees, most fortunate Parīkṣit, you have inquired very nicely, for although constantly hearing the pastimes of the Lord, you are perceiving His activities to be newer and newer.

PURPORT

Unless one is very advanced in Kṛṣṇa consciousness, one cannot stick to hearing the pastimes of the Lord constantly. *Nityaṁ nava-navāya-mānam:* even though advanced devotees hear continually about the Lord for years, they still feel that these topics are coming to them as newer and fresher. Therefore such devotees cannot give up hearing of the pastimes of Lord Kṛṣṇa. *Premāñjana-cchurita-bhakti-vilocanena santaḥ sadaiva hṛdayeṣu vilokayanti.* The word *santaḥ* is used to refer to persons who have developed love for Kṛṣṇa. *Yaṁ śyāmasundaram acintya-guṇa-svarūpaṁ govindam ādi-puruṣaṁ tam ahaṁ bhajāmi* (*Brahma-saṁhitā* 5.38). Parīkṣit Mahārāja, therefore, is addressed as *bhāgavatottama*, the best of devotees, because unless one is very much elevated in devotional service, one cannot feel ecstasy from hearing more and more and appreciate the topics as ever fresher and newer.

TEXT 2

सतामयं सारभृतां निसर्गो
यदर्थवाणीश्रुतिचेतसामपि ।
प्रतिक्षणं नव्यवदच्युतस्य यत्
स्त्रिया विटानामिव साधुवार्ता ॥ २ ॥

satām ayaṁ sāra-bhṛtāṁ nisargo
yad-artha-vāṇī-śruti-cetasām api
prati-kṣaṇaṁ navya-vad acyutasya yat
striyā viṭānām iva sādhu vārtā

satām—of the devotees; *ayam*—this; *sāra-bhṛtām*—those who are *paramahaṁsas*, who have accepted the essence of life; *nisargaḥ*—feature or symptom; *yat*—which; *artha-vāṇī*—the aim of life, the aim of profit; *śruti*—the aim of understanding; *cetasām api*—who have decided to accept the bliss of transcendental subjects as the aim and object of life; *prati-kṣaṇam*—every moment; *navya-vat*—as if newer and newer; *acyutasya*—of Lord Kṛṣṇa; *yat*—because; *striyāḥ*—(topics) of woman or sex; *viṭānām*—of debauchees, who are attached to women; *iva*—exactly like; *sādhu vārtā*—actual conversation.

TRANSLATION

Paramahaṁsas, devotees who have accepted the essence of life, are attached to Kṛṣṇa in the core of their hearts, and He is the aim of their lives. It is their nature to talk only of Kṛṣṇa at every

moment, as if such topics were newer and newer. They are attached to such topics, just as materialists are attached to topics of women and sex.

PURPORT

The word *sāra-bhṛtām* means *paramahaṁsas.* The *haṁsa,* or swan, accepts milk from a mixture of milk and water and rejects the water. Similarly, the nature of persons who have taken to spiritual life and Kṛṣṇa consciousness, understanding Kṛṣṇa to be the life and soul of everyone, is that they cannot give up *kṛṣṇa-kathā,* or topics about Kṛṣṇa, at any moment. Such *paramahaṁsas* always see Kṛṣṇa within the core of the heart (*santaḥ sadaiva hṛdayeṣu vilokayanti*). *Kāma* (desires), *krodha* (anger) and *bhaya* (fear) are always present in the material world, but in the spiritual, or transcendental, world one can use them for Kṛṣṇa. *Kāmaṁ kṛṣṇa-karmārpaṇe.* The desire of the *paramahaṁsas,* therefore, is to act always for Kṛṣṇa. *Krodhaṁ bhakta-dveṣi jane.* They use anger against the nondevotees and transform *bhaya,* or fear, into fear of being deviated from Kṛṣṇa consciousness. In this way, the life of a *paramahaṁsa* devotee is used entirely for Kṛṣṇa, just as the life of a person attached to the material world is used simply for women and money. What is day for the materialistic person is night for the spiritualist. What is very sweet for the materialist—namely women and money—is regarded as poison by the spiritualist.

sandarśanaṁ viṣayiṇām atha yoṣitāṁ ca
ha hanta hanta viṣa-bhakṣaṇato 'py asādhu

This is the instruction of Caitanya Mahāprabhu. For the *paramahaṁsa,* Kṛṣṇa is everything, but for the materialist, women and money are everything.

TEXT 3

शृणुष्वावहितो राजन्नपि गुह्यं वदामि ते ।
ब्रूयुः स्निग्धस्य शिष्यस्य गुरवो गुह्यमप्युत ॥ ३ ॥

śṛṇuṣvāvahito rājann
api guhyam vadāmi te

brūyuḥ snigdhasya śiṣyasya
guravo guhyam apy uta

śṛṇuṣva—please hear; *avahitaḥ*—with great attention; *rājan*—O King (Mahārāja Parīkṣit); *api*—although; *guhyam*—very confidential (because ordinary men cannot understand the activities of Kṛṣṇa); *vadāmi*—I shall explain; *te*—unto you; *brūyuḥ*—explain; *snigdhasya*—submissive; *śiṣyasya*—of a disciple; *guravaḥ*—spiritual masters; *guhyam*—very confidential; *api uta*—even so.

TRANSLATION

O King, kindly hear me with great attention. Although the activities of the Supreme Lord are very confidential, no ordinary man being able to understand them, I shall speak about them to you, for spiritual masters explain to a submissive disciple even subject matters that are very confidential and difficult to understand.

TEXT 4

तथाघवदनान्मृत्यो रक्षित्वा वत्सपालकान् ।
सरित्पुलिनमानीय भगवानिदमब्रवीत् ॥ ४ ॥

tathāgha-vadanān mṛtyo
rakṣitvā vatsa-pālakān
sarit-pulinam ānīya
bhagavān idam abravīt

tathā—thereafter; *agha-vadanāt*—from the mouth of Aghāsura; *mṛtyoḥ*—death personified; *rakṣitvā*—after saving; *vatsa-pālakān*—all the cowherd boys and calves; *sarit-pulinam*—to the bank of the river; *ānīya*—bringing them; *bhagavān*—the Supreme Personality of Godhead, Kṛṣṇa; *idam*—these words; *abravīt*—spoke.

TRANSLATION

Then, after saving the boys and calves from the mouth of Aghāsura, who was death personified, Lord Kṛṣṇa, the Supreme

Personality of Godhead, brought them all to the bank of the river and spoke the following words.

TEXT 5

अहोऽतिरम्यं पुलिनं वयस्याः
स्वकेलिसम्पन्मृदुलाच्छबालुकम् ।
स्फुटत्सरोगन्धहृतालिपत्रिक-
ध्वनिप्रतिध्वानलसद्द्रुमाकुलम् ॥ ५ ॥

aho 'tiramyaṁ pulinaṁ vayasyāḥ
sva-keli-sampan mṛdulāccha-bālukam
sphuṭat-saro-gandha-hṛtāli-patrika-
dhvani-pratidhvāna-lasad-drumākulam

aho—oh; *ati-ramyam*—very, very beautiful; *pulinam*—the bank of the river; *vayasyāḥ*—My dear friends; *sva-keli-sampat*—full with all paraphernalia for pastimes of play; *mṛdula-accha-bālukam*—the very soft and clean sandy bank; *sphuṭat*—in full bloom; *saraḥ-gandha*—by the aroma of the lotus flower; *hṛta*—attracted; *ali*—of the bumblebees; *patrika*—and of the birds; *dhvani-pratidhvāna*—the sounds of their chirping and moving and the echoes of these sounds; *lasat*—moving all over; *druma-ākulam*—full of nice trees.

TRANSLATION

My dear friends, just see how this riverbank is extremely beautiful because of its pleasing atmosphere. And just see how the blooming lotuses are attracting bees and birds by their aroma. The humming and chirping of the bees and birds is echoing throughout the beautiful trees in the forest. Also, here the sands are clean and soft. Therefore, this must be considered the best place for our sporting and pastimes.

PURPORT

The description of Vṛndāvana forest as given herewith was spoken by Kṛṣṇa five thousand years ago, and the same condition prevailed during the time of the Vaiṣṇava *ācāryas* three or four hundred years ago. *Kūjat-kokila-haṁsa-sārasa-gaṇākīrṇe mayūrākule.* Vṛndāvana forest is always filled with the chirping and cooing of birds like cuckoos (*kokila*), ducks (*haṁsa*) and cranes (*sārasa*), and it is also full of peacocks (*mayūrākule*). The same sounds and atmosphere still prevail in the area where our Kṛṣṇa-Balarāma temple is situated. Everyone who visits this temple is pleased to hear the chirping of the birds as described here (*kū-jat-kokila-haṁsa-sārasa*).

TEXT 6

अत्र भोक्तव्यमस्माभिर्दिवारूढं क्षुधार्दिताः ।
वत्साः समीपेऽपः पीत्वा चरन्तु शनकैस्तृणम् ॥६॥

atra bhoktavyam asmābhir
divārūḍhaṁ kṣudhārditāḥ
vatsāḥ samīpe 'paḥ pītvā
carantu śanakais tṛṇam

atra—here, on this spot; *bhoktavyam*—our lunch should be eaten; *asmābhiḥ*—by us; *diva-ārūḍham*—it is very late now; *kṣudhā arditāḥ*—we are fatigued with hunger; *vatsāḥ*—the calves; *samīpe*—nearby; *apaḥ*—water; *pītvā*—after drinking; *carantu*—let them eat; *śanakaiḥ*—slowly; *tṛṇam*—the grasses.

TRANSLATION

I think we should take our lunch here, since we are already hungry because the time is very late. Here the calves may drink water and go slowly here and there and eat the grass.

TEXT 7

तथेति पाययित्वार्भा वत्सानारुध्य शाद्वले ।
मुक्त्वा शिक्यानि बुभुजुः समं भगवता मुदा ॥ ७ ॥

tatheti pāyayitvārbhā
vatsān ārudhya śādvale

muktvā śikyāni bubhujuḥ
samaṁ bhagavatā mudā

tathā iti—as Kṛṣṇa proposed, the other cowherd boys agreed; *pāyayitvā arbhāḥ*—they allowed to drink water; *vatsān*—the calves; *ārudhya*—tying them to the trees, allowed them to eat; *śādvale*—in a place of green, tender grasses; *muktvā*—opening; *śikyāni*—their bags of eatables and other paraphernalia; *bubhujuḥ*—went and enjoyed; *samam*—equally; *bhagavatā*—with the Supreme Personality of Godhead; *mudā*—in transcendental pleasure.

TRANSLATION

Accepting Lord Kṛṣṇa's proposal, the cowherd boys allowed the calves to drink water from the river and then tied them to trees where there was green, tender grass. Then the boys opened their baskets of food and began eating with Kṛṣṇa in great transcendental pleasure.

TEXT 8

कृष्णस्य विष्वक् पुरुराजिमण्डलै-
रभ्याननाः फुल्लदृशो व्रजार्भकाः ।
सहोपविष्टा विपिने विरेजु-
श्छदा यथाम्भोरुहकर्णिकायाः ॥ ८ ॥

kṛṣṇasya viṣvak puru-rāji-maṇḍalair
abhyānanāḥ phulla-dṛśo vrajārbhakāḥ
sahopaviṣṭā vipine virejuś
chadā yathāmbhoruha-karṇikāyāḥ

kṛṣṇasya viṣvak—surrounding Kṛṣṇa; *puru-rāji-maṇḍalaiḥ*—by different encirclements of associates; *abhyānanāḥ*—everyone looking forward to the center, where Kṛṣṇa was sitting; *phulla-dṛśaḥ*—their faces looking very bright because of transcendental pleasure; *vraja-arbhakāḥ*—all the cowherd boys of Vrajabhūmi; *saha-upaviṣṭāḥ*—sitting with Kṛṣṇa; *vipine*—in the forest; *virejuḥ*—so nicely and beautifully made; *chadāḥ*—petals and leaves; *yathā*—just as; *ambhoruha*—of a lotus flower; *karṇikāyāḥ*—of the whorl.

TRANSLATION

Like the whorl of a lotus flower surrounded by its petals and leaves, Kṛṣṇa sat in the center, encircled by lines of His friends, who all looked very beautiful. Every one of them was trying to look forward toward Kṛṣṇa, thinking that Kṛṣṇa might look toward him. In this way they all enjoyed their lunch in the forest.

PURPORT

To a pure devotee, Kṛṣṇa is always visible, as stated in the *Brahma-saṁhitā* (*santaḥ sadaiva hṛdayeṣu vilokayanti*) and as indicated by Kṛṣṇa Himself in *Bhagavad-gītā* (*sarvataḥ pāṇi-pādaṁ tat sarvato 'kṣi-śiro-mukham*). If by accumulating pious activities (*kṛta-puṇya-puñjāḥ*) one is raised to the platform of pure devotional service, Kṛṣṇa is always visible in the core of one's heart. One who has attained such perfection is all-beautiful in transcendental bliss. The present Kṛṣṇa consciousness movement is an attempt to keep Kṛṣṇa in the center, for if this is done all activities will automatically become beautiful and blissful.

TEXT 9

केचित् पुष्पैर्दलैः केचित् पल्लवैरङ्कुरैः फलैः ।
शिग्भिस्त्वग्भिर्दृषद्भिश्च बुभुजुः कृतभाजनाः ॥ ९ ॥

kecit puṣpair dalaiḥ kecit
pallavair aṅkuraiḥ phalaiḥ
śigbhis tvagbhir dṛṣadbhiś ca
bubhujuḥ kṛta-bhājanāḥ

kecit—someone; *puṣpaiḥ*—by flowers; *dalaiḥ*—by nice leaves of flowers; *kecit*—someone; *pallavaiḥ*—on the surface of bunches of leaves; *aṅkuraiḥ*—on the sprouts of flowers; *phalaiḥ*—and some on fruits; *śigbhiḥ*—some actually in the basket or packet; *tvagbhiḥ*—by the bark of trees; *dṛṣadbhiḥ*—on rocks; *ca*—and; *bubhujuḥ*—enjoyed; *kṛta-bhājanāḥ*—as if they had made their plates for eating.

TRANSLATION

Among the cowherd boys, some placed their lunch on flowers, some on leaves, fruits, or bunches of leaves, some actually in their baskets, some on the bark of trees and some on rocks. This is what the children imagined to be their plates as they ate their lunch.

TEXT 10

सर्वे मिथो दर्शयन्तः स्वस्वभोज्यरुचिं पृथक् ।
हसन्तो हासयन्तश्चाभ्यवजह्रुः सहेश्वराः ॥१०॥

sarve mitho darśayantaḥ
sva-sva-bhojya-ruciṁ pṛthak
hasanto hāsayantaś cā-
bhyavajahruḥ saheśvarāḥ

sarve—all the cowherd boys; *mithaḥ*—to one another; *darśayantaḥ*—showing; *sva-sva-bhojya-rucim pṛthak*—different varieties of foodstuffs brought from home, with their separate and different tastes; *hasantaḥ*—after tasting, they were all laughing; *hāsayantaḥ ca*—and making others laugh; *abhyavajahruḥ*—enjoyed lunch; *saha-īśvarāḥ*—along with Kṛṣṇa.

TRANSLATION

All the cowherd boys enjoyed their lunch with Kṛṣṇa, showing one another the different tastes of the different varieties of preparations they had brought from home. Tasting one another's preparations, they began to laugh and make one another laugh.

PURPORT

Sometimes one friend would say, "Kṛṣṇa, see how my food is relishable," and Kṛṣṇa would take some and laugh. Similarly, Balarāma, Sudāmā and other friends would taste one another's food and laugh. In this way, the friends very jubilantly began to eat their respective preparations brought from home.

TEXT 11

बिभ्रद् वेणुं जठरपटयोः शृङ्गवेत्रे च कक्षे
वामे पाणौ मसृणकवलं तत्फलान्यङ्गुलीषु ।
तिष्ठन् मध्येस्वपरिसुहृदो हासयन् नर्मभिः स्वैः
स्वर्गे लोके मिषति बुभुजे यज्ञभुग् बालकेलिः ॥११॥

bibhrad veṇuṁ jaṭhara-paṭayoḥ śṛṅga-vetre ca kakṣe
vāme pāṇau masṛṇa-kavalaṁ tat-phalāny aṅgulīṣu
tiṣṭhan madhye sva-parisuhṛdo hāsayan narmabhiḥ svaiḥ
svarge loke miṣati bubhuje yajña-bhug bāla-keliḥ

bibhrat veṇum—keeping the flute; *jaṭhara-paṭayoḥ*—between the tight clothing and the abdomen; *śṛṅga-vetre*—both the horn bugle and the cow-driving stick; *ca*—also; *kakṣe*—on the waist; *vāme*—on the left-hand side; *pāṇau*—taking in hand; *masṛṇa-kavalam*—very nice food prepared with rice and first-class curd; *tat-phalāni*—suitable pieces of fruit like bael; *aṅgulīṣu*—between the fingers; *tiṣṭhan*—staying in this way; *madhye*—in the middle; *sva-pari-suhṛdaḥ*—His own personal associates; *hāsayan*—making them laugh; *narmabhiḥ*—with joking words; *svaiḥ*—His own; *svarge loke miṣati*—while the inhabitants of the heavenly planets, Svargaloka, were watching this wonderful scene; *bubhuje*—Kṛṣṇa enjoyed; *yajña-bhuk bāla-keliḥ*—although He accepts offerings in *yajña*, for the sake of childhood pastimes He was enjoying foodstuffs very jubilantly with His cowherd boyfriends.

TRANSLATION

Kṛṣṇa is yajña-bhuk—that is, He eats only offerings of yajña—but to exhibit His childhood pastimes, He now sat with His flute tucked between His waist and His tight cloth on His right side and with His horn bugle and cow-driving stick on His left. Holding in His hand a very nice preparation of yogurt and rice, with pieces of suitable fruit between His fingers, He sat like the whorl of a lotus flower, looking forward toward all His friends, personally joking with them and creating jubilant laughter among them as He ate. At

that time, the denizens of heaven were watching, struck with wonder at how the Personality of Godhead, who eats only in yajña, was now eating with His friends in the forest.

PURPORT

When Kṛṣṇa was eating with His cowherd boyfriends, a certain bumblebee came there to take part in the eating. Thus Kṛṣṇa joked, "Why have you come to disturb My *brāhmaṇa* friend Madhumaṅgala? You want to kill a *brāhmaṇa*. This is not good." All the boys would laugh and enjoy, speaking such joking words while eating. Thus the inhabitants of the higher planets were astonished at how the Supreme Personality of Godhead, who eats only when *yajña* is offered, was now eating like an ordinary child with His friends in the forest.

TEXT 12

भारतैवं वत्सपेषु भुञ्जानेष्वच्युतात्मसु ।
वत्सास्त्वन्तर्वने दूरं विविशुस्तृणलोभिताः ॥१२॥

bhārataivaṁ vatsa-peṣu
bhuñjāneṣv acyutātmasu
vatsās tv antar-vane dūraṁ
viviśus tṛṇa-lobhitāḥ

bhārata—O Mahārāja Parīkṣit; *evam*—in this way (while they were enjoying their lunch); *vatsa-peṣu*—along with all the boys tending the calves; *bhuñjāneṣu*—engaged in taking their food; *acyuta-ātmasu*—all of them being very near and dear to Acyuta, Kṛṣṇa; *vatsāḥ*—the calves; *tu*—however; *antaḥ-vane*—within the deep forest; *dūram*—far away; *viviśuḥ*—entered; *tṛṇa-lobhitāḥ*—being allured by green grass.

TRANSLATION

O Mahārāja Parīkṣit, while the cowherd boys, who knew nothing within the core of their hearts but Kṛṣṇa, were thus engaged in eating their lunch in the forest, the calves went far away, deep into the forest, being allured by green grass.

TEXT 13

तान् दृष्ट्वा भयसंत्रस्तानूचे कृष्णोऽस्य भीभयम् ।
मित्राण्याशान्मा विरमतेहानेष्ये वत्सकानहम् ॥१३॥

tān dṛṣṭvā bhaya-santrastān
ūce kṛṣṇo 'sya bhī-bhayam
mitrāṇy āśān mā viramate-
hāneṣye vatsakān aham

tān—that those calves were going away; *dṛṣṭvā*—seeing; *bhaya-santrastān*—to the cowherd boys, who were disturbed by fear that within the dense forest the calves would be attacked by some ferocious animals; *ūce*—Kṛṣṇa said; *kṛṣṇaḥ asya bhī-bhayam*—Kṛṣṇa, who is Himself the fearful element of all kinds of fear (when Kṛṣṇa is present, there is no fear); *mitrāṇi*—My dear friends; *āśāt*—from your enjoyment of eating; *mā viramata*—do not stop; *iha*—in this place, in this spot; *āneṣye*—I shall bring back; *vatsakān*—the calves; *aham*—I.

TRANSLATION

When Kṛṣṇa saw that His friends the cowherd boys were frightened, He, the fierce controller even of fear itself, said, just to mitigate their fear, "My dear friends, do not stop eating. I shall bring your calves back to this spot by personally going after them Myself."

PURPORT

In the presence of Kṛṣṇa's friendship, a devotee cannot have any fear. Kṛṣṇa is the supreme controller, the controller of even death, which is supposed to be the ultimate fear in this material world. *Bhayaṁ dvitīyābhiniveśataḥ syāt* (*Bhāg.* 11.2.37). This fear arises because of lack of Kṛṣṇa consciousness; otherwise there cannot be any fear. For one who has taken shelter of the lotus feet of Kṛṣṇa, this material world of fear becomes hardly dangerous at all.

bhavāmbudhir vatsa-padaṁ paraṁ padaṁ
padaṁ padaṁ yad vipadāṁ na teṣām

Bhavāmbudhiḥ, the material ocean of fear, becomes very easy to cross by the mercy of the supreme controller. This material world, in which there is fear and danger at every step (*padaṁ padaṁ yad vipadām*), is not meant for those who have taken shelter at Kṛṣṇa's lotus feet. Such persons are delivered from this fearful world.

samāśritā ye pada-pallava-plavaṁ
mahat-padaṁ puṇya-yaśo murāreḥ
bhavāmbudhir vatsa-padaṁ paraṁ padaṁ
padaṁ padaṁ yad vipadāṁ na teṣām
(*Bhāg.* 10.14.58)

Everyone, therefore, should take shelter of the Supreme Person, who is the source of fearlessness, and thus be secure.

TEXT 14

इत्युक्त्वाद्रिदरीकुञ्जगह्वरेष्वात्मवत्सकान् ।
विचिन्वन् भगवान् कृष्णः सपाणिकवलो ययौ ॥ १४ ॥

ity uktvādri-darī-kuñja-
gahvareṣv ātma-vatsakān
vicinvan bhagavān kṛṣṇaḥ
sapāṇi-kavalo yayau

iti uktvā—saying this ("Let Me bring your calves personally"); *adri-darī-kuñja-gahvareṣu*—everywhere in the mountains, the mountain caves, the bushes and narrow places; *ātma-vatsakān*—the calves belonging to His own personal friends; *vicinvan*—searching out; *bhagavān*—the Supreme Personality of Godhead; *kṛṣṇaḥ*—Lord Kṛṣṇa; *sa-pāṇi-kavalaḥ*—carrying His yogurt and rice in His hand; *yayau*—started out.

TRANSLATION

"Let Me go and search for the calves," Kṛṣṇa said. "Don't disturb your enjoyment." Then, carrying His yogurt and rice in His hand, the Supreme Personality of Godhead, Kṛṣṇa, immediately went out to search for the calves of His friends. To please His

friends, He began searching in all the mountains, mountain caves, bushes and narrow passages.

PURPORT

The *Vedas* (*Śvetāśvatara Up.* 6.8) assert that the Supreme Personality of Godhead has nothing to do personally (*na tasya kāryaṁ karaṇaṁ ca vidyate*) because He is doing everything through His energies and potencies (*parāsya śaktir vividhaiva śrūyate*). Nonetheless, here we see that He took personal care to find the calves of His friends. This was Kṛṣṇa's causeless mercy. *Mayādhyakṣeṇa prakṛtiḥ sūyate sa-carācaram:* all the affairs of the entire world and the entire cosmic manifestation are working under His direction, through His different energies. Still, when there is a need to take care of His friends, He does this personally. Kṛṣṇa assured His friends, "Don't be afraid. I am going personally to search for your calves." This was Kṛṣṇa's causeless mercy.

TEXT 15

अम्भोजन्मजनिस्तदन्तरगतो मायार्भकस्येशितु-
र्द्रष्टुं मञ्जु महित्वमन्यदपि तद्वत्सानितो वत्सपान् ।
नीत्वान्यत्र कुरूद्वहान्तरदधात् खेऽवस्थितो यः पुरा
दृष्ट्वाघासुरमोक्षणं प्रभवतः प्राप्तः परं विस्मयम् ॥१५॥

ambhojanma-janis tad-antara-gato māyārbhakasyeśitur
draṣṭuṁ mañju mahitvam anyad api tad-vatsān ito vatsapān
nītvānyatra kurūdvahāntaradadhāt khe 'vasthito yaḥ purā
dṛṣṭvāghāsura-mokṣaṇaṁ prabhavataḥ prāptaḥ paraṁ vismayam

ambhojanma-janiḥ—Lord Brahmā, who was born from a lotus flower; *tat-antara-gataḥ*—now became entangled with the affairs of Kṛṣṇa, who was enjoying luncheon pastimes with His cowherd boys; *māyā-arbhakasya*—of the boys made by Kṛṣṇa's *māyā; īśituḥ*—of the supreme controller; *draṣṭum*—just to see; *mañju*—very pleasing; *mahitvam anyat api*—other glories of the Lord also; *tat-vatsān*—their calves; *itaḥ*—than that place where they were; *vatsa-pān*—and the cowherd boys taking care of the calves; *nītvā*—bringing them; *anyatra*—to a different place; *kurūdvaha*—O Mahārāja Parīkṣit; *antara-dadhāt*—kept hidden and invisible for some time; *khe avasthitaḥ yaḥ*—this person Brahmā, who was situated in the higher planetary system in the sky; *purā*—formerly; *dṛṣṭvā*—was observing; *aghāsura-mokṣaṇam*—the wonderful killing and deliverance of Aghāsura from material tribulation; *prabhavataḥ*—of the all-potent Supreme Person; *prāptaḥ param vismayam*—had become extremely astonished.

TRANSLATION

O Mahārāja Parīkṣit, Brahmā, who resides in the higher planetary system in the sky, had observed the activities of the most powerful Kṛṣṇa in killing and delivering Aghāsura, and he was astonished. Now that same Brahmā wanted to show some of his own power and see the power of Kṛṣṇa, who was engaged in His childhood pastimes, playing as if with ordinary cowherd boys. Therefore, in Kṛṣṇa's absence, Brahmā took all the boys and calves to another place. Thus he became entangled, for in the very near future he would see how powerful Kṛṣṇa was.

PURPORT

When Aghāsura was being killed by Kṛṣṇa, who was accompanied by His associates, Brahmā was astonished, but when he saw that Kṛṣṇa was very much enjoying His pastimes of lunch, he was even more astonished and wanted to test whether Kṛṣṇa was actually there. Thus he became entangled in Kṛṣṇa's *māyā*. After all, Brahmā was born materially. As mentioned here, *ambhojanma-janiḥ:* he was born of *ambhoja*, a lotus flower. It does not matter that he was born of a lotus and not of any man, animal or material father. A lotus is also material, and anyone born through the material energy must be subject to the four material deficiencies: *bhrama* (the tendency to commit mistakes), *pramāda* (the tendency to be illusioned), *vipralipsā* (the tendency to cheat) and *karaṇāpāṭava* (imperfect senses). Thus Brahmā also became entangled.

Brahmā, with his *māyā*, wanted to test whether Kṛṣṇa was actually present. These cowherd boys were but expansions of Kṛṣṇa's personal self (*ānanda-cinmaya-rasa-pratibhāvitābhiḥ*). Later Kṛṣṇa would show Brahmā how He expands Himself into everything as His personal pleasure, *ānanda-cinmaya-rasa. Hlādinī śaktir asmāt:* Kṛṣṇa has a transcendental potency called *hlādinī śakti.* He does not enjoy anything that is a product of the material energy. Brahmā, therefore, would see Lord Kṛṣṇa expand His energy.

Brahmā wanted to take away Kṛṣṇa's associates, but instead he took away some other boys and calves. Rāvaṇa wanted to take away Sītā, but that was impossible, and instead he took away a *māyā* Sītā. Similarly, Brahmā took away *māyārbhakāḥ:* boys manifested by Kṛṣṇa's *māyā.* Brahmā could show some extraordinary opulence to the *māyārbhakāḥ;* but he could not show any extraordinary potency to Kṛṣṇa's associates. That he would see in the very near future. *Māyārbhakasya īśituḥ.* This bewilderment, this *māyā,* was caused by the supreme controller, *prabhavataḥ*—the all-potent Supreme Person, Kṛṣṇa—and we shall see the result. Anyone materially born is subject to bewilderment. This pastime is therefore called *brahma-vimohana-līlā,* the pastime of bewildering Brahmā. *Mohitaṁ nābhijānāti mām ebhyaḥ param avyayam* (Bg. 7.13). Materially born persons cannot fully understand Kṛṣṇa. Even the demigods cannot understand Him (*muhyanti yat sūrayaḥ*). *Tene brahmā hṛdā ya ādi-kavaye* (*Bhāg.* 1.1.1). Everyone, from Brahmā down to the small insect, must take lessons from Kṛṣṇa.

TEXT 16

ततो वत्सानदृष्ट्वैत्य पुलिनेऽपि च वत्सपान् ।
उभावपि वने कृष्णो विचिकाय समन्ततः ॥१६॥

tato vatsān adṛṣṭvaitya
puline 'pi ca vatsapān
ubhāv api vane kṛṣṇo
vicikāya samantataḥ

tataḥ—thereafter; *vatsān*—the calves; *adṛṣṭvā*—not seeing there within the forest; *etya*—after; *puline api*—to the bank of the Yamunā; *ca*—also; *vatsapān*—could not see the cowherd boys; *ubhau api*—both of them (the calves and the cowherd boys); *vane*—within the forest; *kṛṣṇaḥ*—Lord Kṛṣṇa; *vicikāya*—searched all over; *samantataḥ*—here and there.

TRANSLATION

Thereafter, when Kṛṣṇa was unable to find the calves, He returned to the bank of the river, but there He was also unable to see the cowherd boys. Thus He began to search for both the calves and the boys, as if He could not understand what had happened.

PURPORT

Kṛṣṇa could immediately understand that Brahmā had taken away both the calves and the boys, but as an innocent child He searched here and there so that Brahmā could not understand Kṛṣṇa's *māyā*. This was all a dramatic performance. A player knows everything, but still he plays on the stage in such a way that others do not understand him.

TEXT 17

काप्यदृष्ट्वान्तर्विपिने वत्सान् पालांश्च विश्ववित् ।
सर्वं विधिकृतं कृष्णः सहसावजगाम ह ॥१७॥

kvāpy adṛṣṭvāntar-vipine
vatsān pālāṁś ca viśva-vit
sarvaṁ vidhi-kṛtaṁ kṛṣṇaḥ
sahasāvajagāma ha

kva api—anywhere; *adṛṣṭvā*—not seeing at all; *antaḥ-vipine*—within the forest; *vatsān*—the calves; *pālān ca*—and their caretakers, the cowherd boys; *viśva-vit*—Kṛṣṇa, who is aware of everything going on throughout the whole cosmic manifestation; *sarvam*—everything; *vidhi-kṛtam*—was executed by Brahmā; *kṛṣṇaḥ*—Lord Kṛṣṇa; *sahasā*—immediately; *avajagāma ha*—could understand.

TRANSLATION

When Kṛṣṇa was unable to find the calves and their caretakers, the cowherd boys, anywhere in the forest, He could suddenly understand that this was the work of Lord Brahmā.

PURPORT

Although Kṛṣṇa is *viśva-vit,* the knower of everything happening in the entire cosmic manifestation, as an innocent child He showed ignorance of Brahmā's actions, although He could immediately understand that these were the doings of Brahmā. This pastime is called *brahma-vimohana,* the bewilderment of Brahmā. Brahmā was already bewildered by Kṛṣṇa's activities as an innocent child, and now he would be further bewildered.

TEXT 18

ततः कृष्णो मुदं कर्तुं तन्मातॄणां च कस्य च ।
उभयायितमात्मानं चक्रे विश्वकृदीश्वरः ॥१८॥

tataḥ kṛṣṇo mudaṁ kartuṁ
tan-mātṝṇāṁ ca kasya ca
ubhayāyitam ātmānaṁ
cakre viśva-kṛd īśvaraḥ

tataḥ—thereafter; *kṛṣṇaḥ*—the Supreme Personality of Godhead; *mudam*—pleasure; *kartum*—to create; *tat-mātṝṇām ca*—of the mothers of the cowherd boys and calves; *kasya ca*—and (the pleasure) of Brahmā; *ubhayāyitam*—expansion, both as the calves and as the cowherd boys; *ātmānam*—Himself; *cakre*—did; *viśva-kṛt īśvaraḥ*—it was not difficult for Him, for He is the creator of the whole cosmic manifestation.

TRANSLATION

Thereafter, just to create pleasure both for Brahmā and for the mothers of the calves and cowherd boys, Kṛṣṇa, the creator of the entire cosmic manifestation, expanded Himself as calves and boys.

PURPORT

Although Brahmā was already entangled in bewilderment, he wanted to show his power to the cowherd boys; but after he took away the boys and their calves and returned to his abode, Kṛṣṇa created further astonishment for Brahmā, and for the mothers of the boys, by establishing the lunch pastimes in the forest again and replacing all the calves and boys, just as they had appeared before. According to the *Vedas, ekaṁ bahu syām:* the Personality of Godhead can become many, many millions upon millions of calves and cowherd boys, as He did to bewilder Brahmā more and more.

TEXT 19

यावद् वत्सपवत्सकाल्पकवपुर्यावत् कराङ्घ्र्यादिकं
यावद् यष्टिविषाणवेणुदलशिग् यावद् विभूषाम्बरम् ।
यावच्छीलगुणाभिधाकृतिवयो यावद् विहारादिकं
सर्वं विष्णुमयं गिरोऽङ्गवदजः सर्वस्वरूपो बभौ ॥१९॥

yāvad vatsapa-vatsakālpaka-vapur yāvat karāṅghry-ādikaṁ
yāvad yaṣṭi-viṣāṇa-veṇu-dala-śig yāvad vibhūṣāmbaram
yāvac chīla-guṇābhidhākṛti-vayo yāvad vihārādikaṁ
sarvaṁ viṣṇumayaṁ giro 'ṅga-vad ajaḥ sarva-svarūpo babhau

yāvat vatsapa—exactly like the cowherd boys; *vatsaka-alpaka-vapuḥ*—and exactly like the tender bodies of the calves; *yāvat kara-aṅghri-ādikam*—exactly to the measurement of their particular varieties of legs and hands; *yāvat yaṣṭi-viṣāṇa-veṇu-dala-śik*—not only like their bodies but exactly like their bugles, flutes, sticks, lunch bags and so on; *yāvat vibhūṣā-ambaram*—exactly like their ornaments and dress in all their varied particulars; *yāvat śīla-guṇa-abhidhā-ākṛti-vayaḥ*—their exact character, habits, features, attributes and explicit bodily features; *yāvat vihāra-ādikam*—exactly according to their tastes or amusements; *sarvam*—everything in detail; *viṣṇu-mayam*—expansions of Vāsudeva, Viṣṇu; *giraḥ aṅga-vat*—voices exactly like theirs; *ajaḥ*—Kṛṣṇa; *sarva-svarūpaḥ babhau*—created everything in detail as Himself, without any change.

TRANSLATION

By His Vāsudeva feature, Kṛṣṇa simultaneously expanded Himself into the exact number of missing cowherd boys and calves,

with their exact bodily features, their particular types of hands, legs and other limbs, their sticks, bugles and flutes, their lunch bags, their particular types of dress and ornaments placed in various ways, their names, ages and forms, and their special activities and characteristics. By expanding Himself in this way, beautiful Kṛṣṇa proved the statement samagra-jagad viṣṇumayam: "Lord Viṣṇu is all-pervading."

PURPORT

As stated in the *Brahma-saṁhitā* (5.33):

advaitam acyutam anādim ananta-rūpam
ādyam purāṇa-puruṣaṁ nava-yauvanaṁ ca

Kṛṣṇa, *paraṁ brahma*, the Supreme Personality of Godhead, is *ādyam*, the beginning of everything; He is *ādi-puruṣam*, the ever-youthful original person. He can expand Himself in more forms than one can imagine, yet He does not fall down from His original form as Kṛṣṇa; therefore He is called Acyuta. This is the Supreme Personality of Godhead. *Sarvaṁ viṣṇumayaṁ jagat. Sarvaṁ khalv idaṁ brahma.* Kṛṣṇa thus proved that He is everything, that He can become everything, but that still He is personally different from everything (*mat-sthāni sarva-bhūtāni na cāhaṁ teṣv avasthitaḥ*). This is Kṛṣṇa, who is understood by *acintya-bhedābheda-tattva* philosophy. *Pūrṇasya pūrṇam ādāya pūrṇam evāvaśiṣyate:* Kṛṣṇa is always complete, and although He can create millions of universes, all of them full in all opulences, He remains as opulent as ever, without any change (*advaitam*). This is explained by different Vaiṣṇava *ācāryas* through philosophies such as *viśuddhādvaita, viśiṣṭādvaita* and *dvaitādvaita.* Therefore one must learn about Kṛṣṇa from the *ācāryas. Ācāryavān puruṣo veda:* one who follows the path of the *ācāryas* knows things as they are. Such a person can know Kṛṣṇa as He is, at least to some extent, and as soon as one understands Kṛṣṇa (*janma karma ca me divyam evaṁ yo vetti tattvataḥ*), one is liberated from material bondage (*tyaktvā dehaṁ punar janma naiti mām eti so 'rjuna*).

TEXT 20

स्वयमात्मात्मगोवत्सान् प्रतिवार्यात्मवत्सपैः ।
क्रीडन्नात्मविहारैश्च सर्वात्मा प्राविशद् व्रजम् ॥२०॥

svayam ātmātma-govatsān
prativāryātma-vatsapaiḥ
krīḍann ātma-vihārais ca
sarvātmā prāviśad vrajam

svayam ātmā—Kṛṣṇa, who is personally the Supreme Soul, the Supersoul; *ātma-go-vatsān*—now expanded into calves that were also He Himself; *prativārya ātma-vatsapaiḥ*—again He Himself was represented as the cowherd boys controlling and commanding the calves; *krīḍan*—thus Himself constituting everything in these transcendental pastimes; *ātma-vihāraiḥ ca*—enjoying Himself by Himself in different ways; *sarva-ātmā*—the Supersoul, Kṛṣṇa; *prāviśat*—entered; *vrajam*—Vrajabhūmi, the land of Mahārāja Nanda and Yaśodā.

TRANSLATION

Now expanding Himself so as to appear as all the calves and cowherd boys, all of them as they were, and at the same time appear as their leader, Kṛṣṇa entered Vrajabhūmi, the land of His father, Nanda Mahārāja, just as He usually did while enjoying their company.

PURPORT

Kṛṣṇa usually stayed in the forest and pasturing ground, taking care of the calves and cows with His associates the cowherd boys. Now that the original group had been taken away by Brahmā, Kṛṣṇa Himself assumed the forms of every member of the group, without anyone's knowledge, even the knowledge of Baladeva, and continued the usual program. He was ordering His friends to do this and that, and He was controlling the calves and going into the forest to search for them when they went astray, allured by new grass, but these calves and boys were He Himself. This was Kṛṣṇa's inconceivable potency. As explained by Śrīla Jīva Gosvāmī, *rādhā kṛṣṇa-praṇaya-vikṛtir hlādinī śaktir asmāt.* Rādhā and

Kṛṣṇa are the same. Kṛṣṇa, by expanding His pleasure potency, becomes Rādhārāṇī. The same pleasure potency (*ānanda-cinmaya-rasa*) was expanded by Kṛṣṇa when He Himself became all the calves and boys and enjoyed transcendental bliss in Vrajabhūmi. This was done by the *yogamāyā* potency and was inconceivable to persons under the potency of *mahāmāyā*.

TEXT 21

तत्तद्वत्सान् पृथङ् नीत्वा तत्तद् गोष्ठे निवेश्य सः ।
तत्तदात्माभवद् राजंस्तत्तत्सद्म प्रविष्टवान् ॥२१॥

tat-tad-vatsān pṛthaṅ nītvā
tat-tad-goṣṭhe niveśya saḥ
tat-tad-ātmābhavad rājaṁs
tat-tat-sadma praviṣṭavān

tat-tat-vatsān—the calves, which belonged to different cows; *pṛthak*—separately; *nītvā*—bringing; *tat-tat-goṣṭhe*—to their respective cow sheds; *niveśya*—entering; *saḥ*—Kṛṣṇa; *tat-tat-ātmā*—as originally different individual souls; *abhavat*—He expanded Himself in that way; *rājan*—O King Parīkṣit; *tat-tat-sadma*—their respective houses; *praviṣṭavān*—entered (Kṛṣṇa thus entered everywhere).

TRANSLATION

O Mahārāja Parīkṣit, Kṛṣṇa, who had divided Himself as different calves and also as different cowherd boys, entered different cow sheds as the calves and then different homes as different boys.

PURPORT

Kṛṣṇa had many, many friends, of whom Śrīdāmā, Sudāmā and Subala were prominent. Thus Kṛṣṇa Himself became Śrīdāmā, Sudāmā and Subala and entered their respective houses with their respective calves.

TEXT 22

तन्मातरो वेणुरवत्वरोत्थिता
उत्थाप्य दोर्भिः परिरभ्य निर्भरम् ।

स्नेहस्नुतस्तन्यपयःसुधासवं
मत्वा परं ब्रह्म सुतानपाययन् ॥२२॥

tan-mātaro veṇu-rava-tvarotthitā
utthāpya dorbhiḥ parirabhya nirbharam
sneha-snuta-stanya-payaḥ-sudhāsavaṁ
matvā paraṁ brahma sutān apāyayan

tat-mātaraḥ—the mothers of the respective cowherd boys; *veṇu-rava*—because of the sounds played on flutes and bugles by the cowherd boys; *tvara*—immediately; *utthitāḥ*—awakened from their respective household duties; *utthāpya*—immediately lifted their respective sons; *dorbhiḥ*—with their two arms; *parirabhya*—embracing; *nirbharam*—without feeling any weight; *sneha-snuta*—which was flowing because of intense love; *stanya-payaḥ*—their breast milk; *sudhā-āsavam*—tasting just like a nectarean beverage; *matvā*—accepting the milk like that; *param*—the Supreme; *brahma*—Kṛṣṇa; *sutān apāyayan*—began to feed their respective sons.

TRANSLATION

The mothers of the boys, upon hearing the sounds of the flutes and bugles being played by their sons, immediately rose from their household tasks, lifted their boys onto their laps, embraced them with both arms and began to feed them with their breast milk, which flowed forth because of extreme love specifically for Kṛṣṇa. Actually Kṛṣṇa is everything, but at that time, expressing extreme love and affection, they took special pleasure in feeding Kṛṣṇa, the Parabrahman, and Kṛṣṇa drank the milk from His respective mothers as if it were a nectarean beverage.

PURPORT

Although all the elderly *gopīs* knew that Kṛṣṇa was the son of mother Yaśodā, they still desired, "If Kṛṣṇa had become my son, I would also have taken care of Him like mother Yaśodā." This was their inner ambition. Now, in order to please them, Kṛṣṇa personally took the role of their sons and fulfilled their desire. They enhanced their special love for

Kṛṣṇa by embracing Him and feeding Him, and Kṛṣṇa tasted their breast milk to be just like a nectarean beverage. While thus bewildering Brahmā, He enjoyed the special transcendental pleasure created by *yogamāyā* between all the other mothers and Himself.

TEXT 23

ततो नृपोन्मर्दनमज्जलेपना-
लङ्कारक्षातिलकाशनादिभिः ।
संलालितः स्वाचरितैः प्रहर्षयन्
सायं गतो यामयमेन माधवः ॥२३॥

tato nṛponmardana-majja-lepanā-
laṅkāra-rakṣā-tilakāśanādibhiḥ
saṁlālitaḥ svācaritaiḥ praharṣayan
sāyaṁ gato yāma-yamena mādhavaḥ

tataḥ—thereafter; *nṛpa*—O King (Mahārāja Parīkṣit); *unmardana*—by massaging them with oil; *majja*—by bathing; *lepana*—by smearing the body with oil and sandalwood pulp; *alaṅkāra*—by decorating with ornaments; *rakṣā*—by chanting protective *mantras; tilaka*—by decorating the body with *tilaka* marks in twelve places; *aśana-ādibhiḥ*—and by feeding them sumptuously; *saṁlālitaḥ*—in this way cared for by the mothers; *sva-ācaritaiḥ*—by their characteristic behavior; *praharṣayan*—making the mothers very much pleased; *sāyam*—evening; *gataḥ*—arrived; *yāma-yamena*—as the time of each activity passed; *mādhavaḥ*—Lord Kṛṣṇa.

TRANSLATION

Thereafter, O Mahārāja Parīkṣit, as required according to the scheduled round of His pastimes, Kṛṣṇa returned in the evening, entered the house of each of the cowherd boys, and engaged exactly like the former boys, thus enlivening their mothers with transcendental pleasure. The mothers took care of the boys by massaging them with oil, bathing them, smearing their bodies with sandalwood pulp, decorating them with ornaments, chanting

protective mantras, decorating their bodies with tilaka and giving them food. In this way, the mothers served Kṛṣṇa personally.

TEXT 24

गावस्ततो गोष्ठमुपेत्य सत्वरं
हुङ्कारघोषैः परिहूतसङ्गतान् ।
स्वकान् स्वकान् वत्सतरानपाययन्
मुहुर्लिहन्त्यः स्रवदौधसं पयः ॥२४॥

gāvas tato goṣṭham upetya satvaraṁ
huṅkāra-ghoṣaiḥ parihūta-saṅgatān
svakān svakān vatsatarān apāyayan
muhur lihantyaḥ sravad audhasaṁ payaḥ

gāvaḥ—the calves; *tataḥ*—thereafter; *goṣṭham*—to the cow sheds; *upetya*—reaching; *satvaram*—very soon; *huṅkāra-ghoṣaiḥ*—by making jubilant mooing sounds; *parihūta-saṅgatān*—to call the cows; *svakān svakān*—following their respective mothers; *vatsatarān*—the respective calves; *apāyayan*—feeding them; *muhuḥ*—again and again; *lihantyaḥ*—licking the calves; *sravat audhasam payaḥ*—abundant milk flowing from their milk bags.

TRANSLATION

Thereafter, all the cows entered their different sheds and began mooing loudly, calling for their respective calves. When the calves arrived, the mothers began licking the calves' bodies again and again and profusely feeding them with the milk flowing from their milk bags.

PURPORT

All the dealings between the calves and their respective mothers taking care of them were enacted by Kṛṣṇa Himself.

TEXT 25

गोगोपीनां मातृतास्मिन्नासीत् स्नेहर्धिकां विना ।
पुरोवदास्वपि हरेस्तोकता मायया विना ॥२५॥

go-gopīnāṁ mātṛtāsminn
āsīt snehardhikāṁ vinā
purovad āsv api hares
tokatā māyayā vinā

go-gopīnām—for both the cows and the *gopīs*, the elderly cowherd women; *mātṛtā*—motherly affection; *asmin*—unto Kṛṣṇa; *āsīt*—there ordinarily was; *sneha*—of affection; *ṛdhikām*—any increase; *vinā*—without; *puraḥ-vat*—like before; *āsu*—there was among the cows and *gopīs; api*—although; *hareḥ*—of Kṛṣṇa; *tokatā*—Kṛṣṇa is my son; *māyayā vinā*—without *māyā.*

TRANSLATION

Previously, from the very beginning, the gopīs had motherly affection for Kṛṣṇa. Indeed, their affection for Kṛṣṇa exceeded even their affection for their own sons. In displaying their affection, they had thus distinguished between Kṛṣṇa and their sons, but now that distinction disappeared.

PURPORT

The distinction between one's own son and another's son is not unnatural. Many elderly women have motherly affection for the sons of others. They observe distinctions, however, between those other sons and their own. But now the elderly *gopīs* could not distinguish between their own sons and Kṛṣṇa, for since their own sons had been taken by Brahmā, Kṛṣṇa had expanded as their sons. Therefore, their extra affection for their sons, who were now Kṛṣṇa Himself, was due to bewilderment resembling that of Brahmā. Previously, the mothers of Śrīdāmā, Sudāmā, Subala and Kṛṣṇa's other friends did not have the same affection for one another's sons, but now the *gopīs* treated all the boys as their own. Śukadeva Gosvāmī, therefore, wanted to explain this increment of affection in terms of Kṛṣṇa's bewilderment of Brahmā, the *gopīs*, the cows and everyone else.

TEXT 26

व्रजौकसां स्वतोकेषु स्नेहवल्ल्याब्दमन्वहम् ।
शनैर्निःसीम ववृधे यथा कृष्णे त्वपूर्ववत् ॥२६॥

vrajaukasāṁ sva-tokeṣu
sneha-vally ābdaṁ anvaham
śanair niḥsīma vavṛdhe
yathā kṛṣṇe tv apūrvavat

vraja-okasām—of all the inhabitants of Vraja, Vṛndāvana; *sva-tokeṣu*—for their own sons; *sneha-vallī*—the creeper of affection; *ā-abdam*—for one year; *anu-aham*—every day; *śanaiḥ*—gradually; *niḥsīma*—without limit; *vavṛdhe*—increased; *yathā kṛṣṇe*—exactly accepting Kṛṣṇa as their son; *tu*—indeed; *apūrva-vat*—as it had not been previously.

TRANSLATION

Although the inhabitants of Vrajabhūmi, the cowherd men and cowherd women, previously had more affection for Kṛṣṇa than for their own children, now, for one year, their affection for their own sons continuously increased, for Kṛṣṇa had now become their sons. There was no limit to the increment of their affection for their sons, who were now Kṛṣṇa. Every day they found new inspiration for loving their children as much as they loved Kṛṣṇa.

TEXT 27

इत्थमात्मात्मनात्मानं वत्सपालमिषेण सः ।
पालयन् वत्सपो वर्षं चिक्रीडे वनगोष्ठयोः ॥२७॥

ittham ātmātmanātmānaṁ
vatsa-pāla-miṣeṇa saḥ
pālayan vatsapo varṣaṁ
cikrīḍe vana-goṣṭhayoḥ

ittham—in this way; *ātmā*—the Supreme Soul, Kṛṣṇa; *ātmanā*—by Himself; *ātmānam*—Himself again; *vatsa-pāla-miṣeṇa*—with the forms of cowherd boys and calves; *saḥ*—Kṛṣṇa Himself; *pālayan*—maintaining; *vatsa-paḥ*—tending the calves; *varṣam*—continuously for one year; *cikrīḍe*—enjoyed the pastimes; *vana-goṣṭhayoḥ*—both in Vṛndāvana and in the forest.

TRANSLATION

In this way, Lord Śrī Kṛṣṇa, having Himself become the cowherd boys and groups of calves, maintained Himself by Himself. Thus He continued His pastimes, both in Vṛndāvana and in the forest, for one year.

PURPORT

Everything was Kṛṣṇa. The calves, the cowherd boys and their maintainer Himself were all Kṛṣṇa. In other words, Kṛṣṇa expanded Himself in varieties of calves and cowherd boys and continued His pastimes uninterrupted for one year. As stated in *Bhagavad-gītā*, Kṛṣṇa's expansion is situated in everyone's heart as the Supersoul. Similarly, instead of expanding Himself as the Supersoul, He expanded Himself as a portion of calves and cowherd boys for one continuous year.

TEXT 28

एकदा चारयन् वत्सान् सरामो वनमाविशत् ।
पञ्चषासु त्रियामासु हायनापूरणीष्वजः ॥२८॥

ekadā cārayan vatsān
sa-rāmo vanam āviśat
pañca-ṣāsu tri-yāmāsu
hāyanāpūraṇīṣv ajaḥ

ekadā—one day; *cārayan vatsān*—while taking care of all the calves; *sa-rāmaḥ*—along with Balarāma; *vanam*—within the forest; *āviśat*—entered; *pañca-ṣāsu*—five or six; *tri-yāmāsu*—nights; *hāyana*—a whole year; *apūraṇīṣu*—not being fulfilled (five or six days before the completion of one year); *ajaḥ*—Lord Śrī Kṛṣṇa.

TRANSLATION

One day, five or six nights before the completion of the year, Kṛṣṇa, tending the calves, entered the forest along with Balarāma.

PURPORT

Up to this time, even Balarāma was captivated by the bewilderment that covered Brahmā. Even Balarāma did not know that all the calves and cowherd boys were expansions of Kṛṣṇa or that He Himself was also an expansion of Kṛṣṇa. This was disclosed to Balarāma just five or six days before the completion of the year.

TEXT 29

ततो विदूराच्चरतो गावो वत्सानुपव्रजम् ।
गोवर्धनाद्रिशिरसि चरन्त्यो ददृशुस्तृणम् ॥२९॥

tato vidūrāc carato
gāvo vatsān upavrajam
govardhanādri-śirasi
carantyo dadṛśus tṛṇam

tataḥ—thereafter; *vidūrāt*—from a not-distant place; *carataḥ*—while pasturing; *gāvaḥ*—all the cows; *vatsān*—and their respective calves; *upavrajam*—also pasturing near Vṛndāvana; *govardhana-adri-śirasi*—on the top of Govardhana Hill; *carantyaḥ*—while pasturing to find; *dadṛśuḥ*—saw; *tṛṇam*—tender grass nearby.

TRANSLATION

Thereafter, while pasturing atop Govardhana Hill, the cows looked down to find some green grass and saw their calves pasturing near Vṛndāvana, not very far away.

TEXT 30

दृष्ट्वाथ तत्स्नेहवशोऽस्मृतात्मा
स गोव्रजोऽत्यात्मपदुर्गमार्गः ।
द्विपात् ककुद्ग्रीव उदास्यपुच्छो-
ऽगाद्धुङ्कृतैरास्नुपया जवेन ॥३०॥

dṛṣṭvātha tat-sneha-vaśo 'smṛtātmā
sa go-vrajo 'tyātmapa-durga-mārgaḥ
dvi-pāt kukud-grīva udāsya-puccho
'gād dhuṅkṛtair āsru-payā javena

dṛṣṭvā—when the cows saw their calves below; *atha*—thereafter; *tat-sneha-vaśaḥ*—because of increased love for the calves; *asmṛta-ātmā*—as if they had forgotten themselves; *saḥ*—that; *go-vrajaḥ*—herd of cows; *ati-ātma-pa-durga-mārgaḥ*—escaping their caretakers because of increased affection for the calves, although the way was very rough and hard; *dvi-pāt*—pairs of legs together; *kakut-grīvaḥ*—their humps moving with their necks; *udāsya-pucchaḥ*—raising their heads and tails; *agāt*—came; *huṅkṛtaiḥ*—lowing very loudly; *āsru-payāḥ*—with milk flowing from the nipples; *javena*—very forcibly.

TRANSLATION

When the cows saw their own calves from the top of Govardhana Hill, they forgot themselves and their caretakers because of increased affection, and although the path was very rough, they ran toward their calves with great anxiety, each running as if with one pair of legs. Their milk bags full and flowing with milk, their heads and tails raised, and their humps moving with their necks, they ran forcefully until they reached their calves to feed them.

PURPORT

Generally the calves and cows are pastured separately. The elderly men take care of the cows, and the small children see to the calves. This time, however, the cows immediately forgot their position as soon as they saw the calves below Govardhana Hill, and they ran with great force, their tails erect and their front and hind legs joined, until they reached their calves.

TEXT 31

समेत्य गावोऽधो वत्सान्वत्सवत्योऽप्यपाययन् ।
गिलन्त्य इव चाङ्गानि लिहन्त्यः स्वौधसं पयः ॥३१॥

sametya gāvo 'dho vatsān
vatsavatyo 'py apāyayan
gilantya iva cāṅgāni
lihantyaḥ svaudhasaṁ payaḥ

sametya—assembling; *gāvaḥ*—all the cows; *adhaḥ*—down at the foot of Govardhana Hill; *vatsān*—all their calves; *vatsa-vatyaḥ*—as if new calves had been born from them; *api*—even though new calves were present; *apāyayan*—fed them; *gilantyaḥ*—swallowing them; *iva*—as if; *ca*—also; *aṅgāni*—their bodies; *lihantyaḥ*—licking as they do when newborn calves are present; *sva-odhasam payaḥ*—their own milk flowing from the milk bags.

TRANSLATION

The cows had given birth to new calves, but while coming down from Govardhana Hill, the cows, because of increased affection for the older calves, allowed the older calves to drink milk from their milk bags and then began licking the calves' bodies in anxiety, as if wanting to swallow them.

TEXT 32

गोपास्तद्रोधनायासमौघ्यलज्जोरुमन्युना ।
दुर्गाध्वकृच्छ्रतोऽभ्येत्य गोवत्सैर्ददृशुः सुतान् ॥३२॥

gopās tad-rodhanāyāsa-
maughya-lajjoru-manyunā
durgādhva-kṛcchrato 'bhyetya
go-vatsair dadṛśuḥ sutān

gopāḥ—the cowherd men; *tat-rodhana-āyāsa*—of their attempt to stop the cows from going to their calves; *maughya*—on account of the frustration; *lajjā*—being ashamed; *uru-manyunā*—and at the same time becoming very angry; *durga-adhva-kṛcchrataḥ*—although they passed the very rough way with great difficulty; *abhyetya*—after reaching there; *go-vatsaiḥ*—along with the calves; *dadṛśuḥ*—saw; *sutān*—their respective sons.

TRANSLATION

The cowherd men, having been unable to check the cows from going to their calves, felt simultaneously ashamed and angry. They

crossed the rough road with great difficulty, but when they came down and saw their own sons, they were overwhelmed by great affection.

PURPORT

Everyone was increasing in affection for Kṛṣṇa. When the cowherd men coming down from the hill saw their own sons, who were no one else than Kṛṣṇa, their affection increased.

TEXT 33

तदीक्षणोत्प्रेमरसाप्लुताशया
जातानुरागा गतमन्यवोऽर्भकान् ।
उदुह्य दोर्भिः परिरभ्य मूर्धनि
घ्राणैरवापुः परमां मुदं ते ॥३३॥

tad-īkṣaṇotprema-rasāplutāśayā
jātānurāgā gata-manyavo 'rbhakān
uduhya dorbhiḥ parirabhya mūrdhani
ghrāṇair avāpuḥ paramāṁ mudaṁ te

tat-īkṣaṇa-utprema-rasa-āpluta-āśayāḥ—all the thoughts of the cowherd men merged in the mellow of paternal love, which was aroused by seeing their sons; *jāta-anurāgāḥ*—experiencing a great longing or attraction; *gata-manyavaḥ*—their anger disappeared; *arbhakān*—their young sons; *uduhya*—lifting; *dorbhiḥ*—with their arms; *parirabhya*—embracing; *mūrdhani*—on the head; *ghrāṇaiḥ*—by smelling; *avāpuḥ*—obtained; *paramām*—the highest; *mudam*—pleasure; *te*—those cowherd men.

TRANSLATION

At that time, all the thoughts of the cowherd men merged in the mellow of paternal love, which was aroused by the sight of their sons. Experiencing a great attraction, their anger completely disappearing, they lifted their sons, embraced them in their arms and enjoyed the highest pleasure by smelling their sons' heads.

PURPORT

After Brahmā stole the original cowherd boys and calves, Kṛṣṇa expanded Himself to become the boys and calves again. Therefore, because the boys were actually Kṛṣṇa's expansions, the cowherd men were especially attracted to them. At first the cowherd men, who were on top of the hill, were angry, but because of Kṛṣṇa the boys were extremely attractive, and therefore the cowherd men immediately came down from the hill with special affection.

TEXT 34

ततः प्रवयसो गोपास्तोकाश्लेषसुनिर्वृताः ।
कृच्छ्राच्छनैरपगतास्तदनुस्मृत्युदश्रवः ॥३४॥

tataḥ pravayaso gopās
tokāśleṣa-sunirvṛtāḥ
kṛcchrāc chanair apagatās
tad-anusmṛty-udaśravaḥ

tataḥ—thereafter; *pravayasaḥ*—elderly; *gopāḥ*—cowherd men; *toka-āśleṣa-sunirvṛtāḥ*—became overjoyed by embracing their sons; *kṛc-chrāt*—with difficulty; *śanaiḥ*—gradually; *apagatāḥ*—ceased from that embracing and returned to the forest; *tat-anusmṛti-uda-śravaḥ*—as they remembered their sons, tears began to roll down from their eyes.

TRANSLATION

Thereafter the elderly cowherd men, having obtained great feeling from embracing their sons, gradually and with great difficulty and reluctance ceased embracing them and returned to the forest. But as the men remembered their sons, tears began to roll down from their eyes.

PURPORT

In the beginning the cowherd men were angry that the cows were being attracted by the calves, but when the men came down from the hill, they themselves were attracted by their sons, and therefore the men embraced them. To embrace one's son and smell his head are symptoms of affection.

TEXT 35

व्रजस्य रामः प्रेमर्धेर्वीक्ष्यौत्कण्ठ्यमनुक्षणम् ।
मुक्तस्तनेष्वपत्येष्वप्यहेतुविदचिन्तयत् ॥३५॥

vrajasya rāmaḥ premardher
vīkṣyautkaṇṭhyam anukṣaṇam
mukta-staneṣv apatyeṣv apy
ahetu-vid acintayat

vrajasya—of the herd of cows; *rāmaḥ*—Balarāma; *prema-ṛdheḥ*—because of an increase of affection; *vīkṣya*—after observing; *autkaṇṭhyam*—attachment; *anu-kṣaṇam*—constantly; *mukta-staneṣu*—who had grown up and were no longer drawing milk from their mothers; *apatyeṣu*—in regard to those calves; *api*—even; *ahetu-vit*—not understanding the reason; *acintayat*—began to consider as follows.

TRANSLATION

Because of an increase of affection, the cows had constant attachment even to those calves that were grown up and had stopped sucking milk from their mothers. When Baladeva saw this attachment, He was unable to understand the reason for it, and thus He began to consider as follows.

PURPORT

The cows had younger calves who had started sucking milk from their mothers, and some of the cows had newly given birth, but now, because of love, the cows enthusiastically showed their affection for the older calves, which had left off milking. These calves were grown up, but still the mothers wanted to feed them. Therefore Balarāma was a little surprised, and He wanted to inquire from Kṛṣṇa about the reason for their behavior. The mothers were actually more anxious to feed the older calves, although the new calves were present, because the older calves were expansions of Kṛṣṇa. These surprising events were taking place by the manipulation of *yogamāyā*. There are two *māyās* working under the direction of Kṛṣṇa—*mahāmāyā*, the energy of the material world, and *yogamāyā*, the energy of the spiritual world. These uncommon events were taking place because of the influence of *yogamāyā*. From the very day on which Brahmā stole the calves and boys, *yogamāyā* acted in such a way that the residents of Vṛndāvana, including even Lord Balarāma, could not understand how *yogamāyā* was working and causing such uncommon things to happen. But as *yogamāyā* gradually acted, Balarāma in particular was able to understand what was happening, and therefore He inquired from Kṛṣṇa.

TEXT 36

किमेतदद्भुतमिव वासुदेवेऽखिलात्मनि ।
व्रजस्य सात्मनस्तोकेष्वपूर्वं प्रेम वर्धते ॥३६॥

kim etad adbhutam iva
vāsudeve 'khilātmani
vrajasya sātmanas tokeṣv
apūrvaṁ prema vardhate

kim—what; *etat*—this; *adbhutam*—wonderful; *iva*—just as; *vāsudeve*—in Vāsudeva, Lord Śrī Kṛṣṇa; *akhila-ātmani*—the Supersoul of all living entities; *vrajasya*—of all the inhabitants of Vraja; *sa-ātmanaḥ*—along with Me; *tokeṣu*—in these boys; *apūrvam*—unprecedented; *prema*—affection; *vardhate*—is increasing.

TRANSLATION

What is this wonderful phenomenon? The affection of all the inhabitants of Vraja, including Me, toward these boys and calves is increasing as never before, just like our affection for Lord Kṛṣṇa, the Supersoul of all living entities.

PURPORT

This increase of affection was not *māyā;* rather, because Kṛṣṇa had expanded Himself as everything and because the whole life of everyone in Vṛndāvana was meant for Kṛṣṇa, the cows, because of affection for Kṛṣṇa, had more affection for the older calves than for the new calves, and the men increased in their affection for their sons. Balarāma was astonished to see all the residents of Vṛndāvana so affectionate toward their own children, exactly as they had been for Kṛṣṇa. Similarly, the cows had grown affectionate toward their calves—as much as toward Kṛṣṇa. Balarāma was surprised to see the acts of *yogamāyā.* Therefore He inquired from Kṛṣṇa, "What is happening here? What is this mystery?"

TEXT 37

केयं वा कुत आयाता दैवी वा नार्युतासुरी ।
प्रायो मायास्तु मे भर्तुर्नान्या मेऽपि विमोहिनी ॥३७॥

keyaṁ vā kuta āyātā
daivī vā nāry utāsurī
prāyo māyāstu me bhartur
nānyā me 'pi vimohinī

kā—who; *iyam*—this; *vā*—or; *kutaḥ*—from where; *āyātā*—has come; *daivī*—whether demigod; *vā*—or; *nārī*—woman; *uta*—or; *āsurī*—demoness; *prāyaḥ*—in most cases; *māyā*—illusory energy; *astu*—she must be; *me*—My; *bhartuḥ*—of the master, Lord Kṛṣṇa; *na*—not; *anyā*—any other; *me*—My; *api*—certainly; *vimohinī*—bewilderer.

TRANSLATION

Who is this mystic power, and where has she come from? Is she a demigod or a demoness? She must be the illusory energy of My master, Lord Kṛṣṇa, for who else can bewilder Me?

PURPORT

Balarāma was surprised. This extraordinary show of affection, He thought, was something mystical, performed either by the demigods or some wonderful man. Otherwise, how could this wonderful change take place? "This *māyā* might be some *rākṣasī-māyā,*" He thought, "but how can *rākṣasī-māyā* have any influence upon Me? This is not possible. Therefore it must be the *māyā* of Kṛṣṇa." He thus concluded that the mystical change must have been caused by Kṛṣṇa, whom Balarāma considered His worshipable Personality of Godhead. He thought, "It was arranged by Kṛṣṇa, and even I could not check its mystic power." Thus Balarāma understood that all these boys and calves were only expansions of Kṛṣṇa.

TEXT 38

इति सञ्चिन्त्य दाशार्हो वत्सान् सवयसानपि ।
सर्वानाचष्ट वैकुण्ठं चक्षुषा वयुनेन सः ॥३८॥

iti sañcintya dāśārho
vatsān sa-vayasān api
sarvān ācaṣṭa vaikuṇṭhaṁ
cakṣuṣā vayunena saḥ

iti sañcintya—thinking in this way; *dāśārhaḥ*—Baladeva; *vatsān*—the calves; *sa-vayasān*—along with His companions; *api*—also; *sarvān*—all; *ācaṣṭa*—saw; *vaikuṇṭham*—as Śrī Kṛṣṇa only; *cakṣuṣā vayunena*—with the eye of transcendental knowledge; *saḥ*—He (Baladeva).

TRANSLATION

Thinking in this way, Lord Balarāma was able to see, with the eye of transcendental knowledge, that all these calves and Kṛṣṇa's friends were expansions of the form of Śrī Kṛṣṇa.

PURPORT

Every individual is different. There are even differences between twin brothers. Yet when Kṛṣṇa expanded Himself as the boys and calves, each boy and each calf appeared in its own original feature, with the same individual way of acting, the same tendencies, the same color, the same dress, and so on, for Kṛṣṇa manifested Himself with all these differences. This was Kṛṣṇa's opulence.

TEXT 39

नैते सुरेशा ऋषयो न चैते
त्वमेव भासीश भिदाश्रयेऽपि ।
सर्वं पृथक्त्वं निगमात् कथं वदे-
त्युक्तेन वृत्तं प्रभुणा बलोऽवैत् ॥३९॥

naite sureśā ṛṣayo na caite
tvam eva bhāsīśa bhid-āśraye 'pi

sarvaṁ pṛthak tvaṁ nigamāt kathaṁ vadety
uktena vṛttaṁ prabhuṇā balo 'vait

na—not; *ete*—these boys; *sura-īśāḥ*—the best of the demigods; *ṛṣayaḥ*—great sages; *na*—not; *ca*—and; *ete*—these calves; *tvam*—You (Kṛṣṇa); *eva*—alone; *bhāsi*—are manifesting; *īśa*—O supreme controller; *bhit-āśraye*—in the existence of varieties of difference; *api*—even; *sarvam*—everything; *pṛthak*—existing; *tvam*—You (Kṛṣṇa); *nigamāt*—briefly; *katham*—how; *vada*—please explain; *iti*—thus; *uktena*—having been requested (by Baladeva); *vṛttam*—the situation; *prabhuṇā*—(having been explained) by Lord Kṛṣṇa; *balaḥ*—Baladeva; *avait*—understood.

TRANSLATION

Lord Baladeva said, "O supreme controller! These boys are not great demigods, as I previously thought. Nor are these calves great sages like Nārada. Now I can see that You alone are manifesting Yourself in all varieties of difference. Although one, You are existing in the different forms of the calves and boys. Please briefly explain this to Me." Having thus been requested by Lord Baladeva, Kṛṣṇa explained the whole situation, and Baladeva understood it.

PURPORT

Inquiring from Kṛṣṇa about the actual situation, Lord Balarāma said, "My dear Kṛṣṇa, in the beginning I thought that all these cows, calves and cowherd boys were either great sages and saintly persons or demigods, but at the present it appears that they are actually Your expansions. They are all You; You Yourself are playing as the calves and cows and boys. What is the mystery of this situation? Where have those other calves and cows and boys gone? And why are You expanding Yourself as the cows, calves and boys? Will You kindly tell Me what is the cause?" At the request of Balarāma, Kṛṣṇa briefly explained the whole situation: how the calves and boys were stolen by Brahmā and how He was concealing the incident by expanding Himself so that people would not know that the original cows, calves and boys were missing. Balarāma understood, therefore, that this was not *māyā* but Kṛṣṇa's opulence. Kṛṣṇa has all opulences, and this was but another opulence of Kṛṣṇa.

"At first," Lord Balarāma said, "I thought that these boys and calves were a display of the power of great sages like Nārada, but now I see that all these boys and calves are You." After inquiring from Kṛṣṇa, Lord Balarāma understood that Kṛṣṇa Himself had become many. That the Lord can do this is stated in the *Brahma-saṁhitā* (5.33). *Advaitam acyutam anādim ananta-rūpam:* although He is one, He can expand Himself in so many forms. According to the Vedic version, *ekaṁ bahu syām:* He can expand Himself into many thousands and millions but still remain one. In that sense, everything is spiritual because everything is an expansion of Kṛṣṇa; that is, everything is an expansion either of Kṛṣṇa Himself or of His potency. Because the potency is nondifferent from the potent, the potency and the potent are one (*śakti-śaktimator abhedaḥ*). The Māyāvādīs, however, say, *cid-acit-samanvayaḥ:* spirit and matter are one. This is a wrong conception. Spirit (*cit*) is different from matter (*acit*), as explained by Kṛṣṇa Himself in *Bhagavad-gītā* (7.4–5):

bhūmir āpo 'nalo vāyuḥ
khaṁ mano buddhir eva ca
ahaṅkāra itīyaṁ me
bhinnā prakṛtir aṣṭadhā

apareyam itas tv anyāṁ
prakṛtiṁ viddhi me parām
jīva-bhūtāṁ mahā-bāho
yayedaṁ dhāryate jagat

"Earth, water, fire, air, ether, mind, intelligence and false ego—all together these eight comprise My separated material energies. But besides this inferior nature, O mighty-armed Arjuna, there is a superior energy of Mine, which consists of all living entities who are struggling with material nature and are sustaining the universe." Spirit and matter cannot be made one, for actually they are superior and inferior energies, yet the Māyāvādīs, or Advaita-vādīs, try to make them one. This is wrong. Although spirit and matter ultimately come from the same one source, they cannot be made one. For example, there are many things that come from our bodies, but although they come from the same source, they cannot be made one. We should be careful to note that although the supreme source is one, the emanations from this source should be separately regarded as inferior and superior. The difference between the Māyāvāda and Vaiṣṇava philosophies is that the Vaiṣṇava philosophy recognizes this fact. Śrī Caitanya Mahāprabhu's philosophy, therefore, is called *acintya-bhedābheda*—simultaneous oneness and difference. For example, fire and heat cannot be separated, for where there is fire there is heat and where there is heat there is fire. Nonetheless, although we cannot touch fire, heat we can tolerate. Therefore, although they are one, they are different.

TEXT 40

तावदेत्यात्मभूरात्ममानेन त्रुट्यनेहसा ।
पुरोवदाब्दं क्रीडन्तं ददृशे सकलं हरिम् ॥४०॥

tāvad etyātmabhūr ātma-
mānena truṭy-anehasā
purovad ābdaṁ krīḍantaṁ
dadṛśe sa-kalaṁ harim

tāvat—for so long; *etya*—after returning; *ātma-bhūḥ*—Lord Brahmā; *ātma-mānena*—by his (Brahmā's) own measurement; *truṭi-anehasā*—by a moment's time; *puraḥ-vat*—just as previously; *ā-abdam*—for one year (by human measurement of time); *krīḍantam*—playing; *dadṛśe*—he saw; *sa-kalam*—along with His expansions; *harim*—Lord Hari (Śrī Kṛṣṇa).

TRANSLATION

When Lord Brahmā returned after a moment of time had passed (according to his own measurement), he saw that although by human measurement a complete year had passed, Lord Kṛṣṇa, after all that time, was engaged just as before in playing with the boys and calves, who were His expansions.

PURPORT

Lord Brahmā had gone away for only a moment of his time, but when he returned, a year of human time had passed. On different planets, the calculation of time is different. To give an example, a man-made satellite may orbit the earth in an hour and twenty-five minutes and thus complete one full day, although a day ordinarily takes twenty-four hours for those living on earth. Therefore, what was but a moment for Brahmā was one year on earth. Kṛṣṇa continued to expand Himself in so many forms for one year, but by the arrangement of *yogamāyā* no one could understand this but Balarāma.

After one moment of Brahmā's calculation, Brahmā came back to see the fun caused by his stealing the boys and calves. But he was also afraid that he was playing with fire. Kṛṣṇa was his master, and he had played mischief for fun by taking away Kṛṣṇa's calves and boys. He was really anxious, so he did not stay away very long; he came back after a moment (of his calculation). When Brahmā returned, he saw that all the boys, calves and cows were playing with Kṛṣṇa in the same way as when he had come upon them; by Kṛṣṇa's display of *yogamāyā*, the same pastimes were going on without any change.

On the day when Lord Brahmā had first come, Baladeva could not go with Kṛṣṇa and the cowherd boys, for it was His birthday, and His mother had kept Him back for the proper ceremonial bath, called *śāntika-snāna.* Therefore Lord Baladeva was not taken by Brahmā at that time. Now, one year later, Brahmā returned, and because he returned on exactly the same day, Baladeva was again kept at home for His birthday. Therefore, although this verse mentions that Brahmā saw Kṛṣṇa and all the cowherd boys, Baladeva is not mentioned. It was five or six days earlier that Baladeva had inquired from Kṛṣṇa about the extraordinary affection of the cows and cowherd men, but now, when Brahmā returned, Brahmā saw all the calves and cowherd boys playing with Kṛṣṇa as expansions of Kṛṣṇa, but he did not see Baladeva. As in the previous year, Lord Baladeva did not go to the woods on the day Lord Brahmā appeared there.

TEXT 41

यावन्तो गोकुले बालाः सवत्साः सर्व एव हि ।
मायाशये शयाना मे नाद्यापि पुनरुत्थिताः ॥४१॥

yāvanto gokule bālāḥ
sa-vatsāḥ sarva eva hi

māyāśaye śayānā me
nādyāpi punar utthitāḥ

yāvantaḥ—whatsoever, as many as; *gokule*—in Gokula; *bālāḥ*—boys; *sa-vatsāḥ*—along with their calves; *sarve*—all; *eva*—indeed; *hi*—because; *māyā-āśaye*—on the bed of *māyā; śayānāḥ*—are sleeping; *me*—my; *na*—not; *adya*—today; *api*—even; *punaḥ*—again; *utthitāḥ*—have risen.

TRANSLATION

Lord Brahmā thought: Whatever boys and calves there were in Gokula, I have kept them sleeping on the bed of my mystic potency, and to this very day they have not yet risen again.

PURPORT

For one year Lord Brahmā kept the calves and boys lying down in a cave by his mystic power. Therefore when Brahmā saw Lord Kṛṣṇa still playing with all the cows and calves, he began trying to reason about what was happening. "What is this?" he thought. "Maybe I took those calves and cowherd boys away but now they have been taken from that cave. Is this what has happened? Has Kṛṣṇa brought them back here?" Then, however, Lord Brahmā saw that the calves and boys he had taken were still in the same mystic *māyā* into which he had put them. Thus he concluded that the calves and cowherd boys now playing with Kṛṣṇa were different from the ones in the cave. He could understand that although the original calves and boys were still in the cave where he had put them, Kṛṣṇa had expanded Himself and so the present demonstration of calves and boys consisted of expansions of Kṛṣṇa. They had the same features, the same mentality and the same intentions, but they were all Kṛṣṇa.

TEXT 42

इत एतेऽत्र कुत्रत्या मन्मायामोहितेतरे ।
तावन्त एव तत्राब्दं क्रीडन्तो विष्णुना समम् ॥४२॥

ita ete 'tra kutratyā
man-māyā-mohitetare

tāvanta eva tatrābdaṁ
krīḍanto viṣṇunā samam

itaḥ—for this reason; *ete*—these boys with their calves; *atra*—here; *kutratyāḥ*—where have they come from; *mat-māyā-mohita-itare*—different from those who were mystified by my illusory potency; *tāvantaḥ*—the same number of boys; *eva*—indeed; *tatra*—there; *ā-abdam*—for one year; *krīḍantaḥ*—are playing; *viṣṇunā samam*—along with Kṛṣṇa.

TRANSLATION

A similar number of boys and calves have been playing with Kṛṣṇa for one whole year, yet they are different from the ones illusioned by my mystic potency. Who are they? Where did they come from?

PURPORT

Although appearing like calves, cows and cowherd boys, these were all Viṣṇu. Actually they were *viṣṇu-tattva*, not *jīva-tattva*. Brahmā was surprised. "The original cowherd boys and cows," he thought, "are still where I put them last year. So who is it that is now keeping company with Kṛṣṇa exactly as before? Where have they come from?" Brahmā was surprised that his mystic power had been neglected. Without touching the original cows and cowherd boys kept by Brahmā, Kṛṣṇa had created another assembly of calves and boys, who were all expansions of *viṣṇu-tattva*. Thus Brahmā's mystic power was superseded.

TEXT 43

एवमेतेषु भेदेषु चिरं ध्यात्वा स आत्मभूः ।
सत्याः के कतरे नेति ज्ञातुं नेष्टे कथञ्चन ॥४३॥

evam eteṣu bhedeṣu
ciraṁ dhyātvā sa ātma-bhūḥ
satyāḥ ke katare neti
jñātuṁ neṣṭe kathañcana

evam—in this way; *eteṣu bhedeṣu*—between these boys, who were existing separately; *ciram*—for a long time; *dhyātvā*—after thinking; *saḥ*—he; *ātma-bhūḥ*—Lord Brahmā; *satyāḥ*—real; *ke*—who; *katare*—who; *na*—are not; *iti*—thus; *jñātum*—to understand; *na*—not; *iṣṭe*—was able; *kathañcana*—in any way at all.

TRANSLATION

Thus Lord Brahmā, thinking and thinking for a long time, tried to distinguish between those two sets of boys, who were each separately existing. He tried to understand who was real and who was not real, but he couldn't understand at all.

PURPORT

Brahmā was puzzled. "The original boys and calves are still sleeping as I have kept them," he thought, "but another set is here playing with Kṛṣṇa. How has this happened?" Brahmā could not grasp what was happening. Which boys were real, and which were not real? Brahmā was unable to come to any definite conclusion. He pondered the matter for a long while. "How can there be two sets of calves and boys at the same time? Have the boys and calves here been created by Kṛṣṇa, or has Kṛṣṇa created the ones lying asleep? Or are both merely creations of Kṛṣṇa?" Brahmā thought about the subject in many different ways. "After I go to the cave and see that the boys and calves are still there, does Kṛṣṇa go take them away and put them here so that I come here and see them, and does Kṛṣṇa then take them from here and put them there?" Brahmā could not figure out how there could be two sets of calves and cowherd boys exactly alike. Although thinking and thinking, he could not understand at all.

TEXT 44

एवं सम्मोहयन् विष्णुं विमोहं विश्वमोहनम् ।
स्वयैव माययाजोऽपि स्वयमेव विमोहितः ॥४४॥

evaṁ sammohayan viṣṇuṁ
vimohaṁ viśva-mohanam

svayaiva māyayājo 'pi
svayam eva vimohitaḥ

evam—in this way; *sammohayan*—wanting to mystify; *viṣṇum*—the all-pervading Lord Kṛṣṇa; *vimoham*—who can never be mystified; *viśva-mohanam*—but who mystifies the entire universe; *svayā*—by his (Brahmā's) own; *eva*—indeed; *māyayā*—by mystic power; *ajaḥ*—Lord Brahmā; *api*—even; *svayam*—himself; *eva*—certainly; *vimohitaḥ*—was put into bewilderment, became mystified.

TRANSLATION

Thus because Lord Brahmā wanted to mystify the all-pervading Lord Kṛṣṇa, who can never be mystified, but who, on the contrary, mystifies the entire universe, he himself was put into bewilderment by his own mystic power.

PURPORT

Brahmā wanted to bewilder Kṛṣṇa, who bewilders the entire universe. The whole universe is under Kṛṣṇa's mystic power (*mama māyā duratyayā*), but Brahmā wanted to mystify Him. The result was that Brahmā himself was mystified, just as one who wants to kill another may himself be killed. In other words, Brahmā was defeated by his own attempt. In a similar position are the scientists and philosophers who want to overcome the mystic power of Kṛṣṇa. They challenge Kṛṣṇa, saying, "What is God? We can do this, and we can do that." But the more they challenge Kṛṣṇa in this way, the more they are implicated in suffering. The lesson here is that we should not try to overcome Kṛṣṇa. Rather, instead of endeavoring to surpass Him, we should surrender to Him (*sarva-dharmān parityajya mām ekaṁ śaraṇaṁ vraja*).

Instead of defeating Kṛṣṇa, Brahmā himself was defeated, for he could not understand what Kṛṣṇa was doing. Since Brahmā, the chief person within this universe, was so bewildered, what is to be said of so-called scientists and philosophers? *Sarva-dharmān parityajya mām ekaṁ śaraṇaṁ vraja.* We should give up all our tiny efforts to defy the arrangement of Kṛṣṇa. Instead, whatever arrangements He proposes, we should accept. This is always better, for this will make us happy. The more we try to defeat the arrangement of Kṛṣṇa, the more we become implicated in Kṛṣṇa's *māyā* (*daivī hy eṣā guṇamayī mama māyā duratyayā*). But one who has reached the point of surrendering to the instructions of Kṛṣṇa (*mām eva ye prapadyante*) is liberated, free from *kṛṣṇa-māyā* (*māyām etāṁ taranti te*). The power of Kṛṣṇa is just like a government that cannot be overcome. First of all there are laws, and then there is police power, and beyond that is military power. Therefore, what is the use of trying to overcome the power of the government? Similarly, what is the use of trying to challenge Kṛṣṇa?

From the next verse it is clear that Kṛṣṇa cannot be defeated by any kind of mystic power. If one gets even a little power of scientific knowledge, one tries to defy God, but actually no one is able to bewilder Kṛṣṇa. When Brahmā, the chief person within the universe, tried to bewilder Kṛṣṇa, he himself was bewildered and astonished. This is the position of the conditioned soul. Brahmā wanted to mystify Kṛṣṇa, but he himself was mystified.

The word *viṣṇum* is significant in this verse. Viṣṇu pervades the entire material world, whereas Brahmā merely occupies one subordinate post.

yasyaika-niśvasita-kālam athāvalambya
jīvanti loma-vila-jā jagadaṇḍa-nāthāḥ
(*Brahma-saṁhitā* 5.48)

The word *nāthāḥ*, which refers to Lord Brahmā, is plural because there are innumerable universes and innumerable Brahmās. Brahmā is but a tiny force. This was exhibited in Dvārakā when Kṛṣṇa called for Brahmā. One day when Brahmā came to see Kṛṣṇa at Dvārakā, the doorman, at Lord Kṛṣṇa's request, asked, "Which Brahmā are you?" Later, when Brahmā inquired from Kṛṣṇa whether this meant that there was more than one Brahmā, Kṛṣṇa smiled and at once called for many Brahmās from many universes. The four-headed Brahmā of this universe then saw innumerable other Brahmās coming to see Kṛṣṇa and offer their respects. Some of them had ten heads, some had twenty, some had a hundred and some had a million heads. Upon seeing this wonderful exhibition, the four-headed Brahmā became nervous and began to think of himself as no more than a mosquito in the midst of many elephants. Therefore, what can Brahmā do to bewilder Kṛṣṇa?

TEXT 45

तम्यां तमोवन्नैहारं खद्योतार्चिरिवाहनि ।
महतीतरमायैश्यं निहन्त्यात्मनि युञ्जतः ॥४५॥

tamyāṁ tamovan naihāraṁ
khadyotārcir ivāhani
mahatītara-māyaiśyaṁ
nihanty ātmani yuñjataḥ

tamyām—on a dark night; *tamaḥ-vat*—just as darkness; *naihāram*—produced by snow; *khadyota-arciḥ*—the light of a glowworm; *iva*—just as; *ahani*—in the daytime, in the sunlight; *mahati*—in a great personality; *itara-māyā*—inferior mystic potency; *aiśyam*—the ability; *nihanti*—destroys; *ātmani*—in his own self; *yuñjataḥ*—of the person who attempts to use.

TRANSLATION

As the darkness of snow on a dark night and the light of a glowworm in the light of day have no value, the mystic power of an inferior person who tries to use it against a person of great power is unable to accomplish anything; instead, the power of that inferior person is diminished.

PURPORT

When one wants to supersede a superior power, one's own inferior power becomes ludicrous. Just as a glowworm in the daytime and snow at night have no value, Brahmā's mystic power became worthless in the presence of Kṛṣṇa, for greater mystic power condemns inferior mystic power. On a dark night, the darkness produced by snow has no meaning. The glowworm appears very important at night, but in the daytime its glow has no value; whatever little value it has is lost. Similarly, Brahmā became insignificant in the presence of Kṛṣṇa's mystic power. Kṛṣṇa's *māyā* was not diminished in value, but Brahmā's *māyā* was condemned. Therefore, one should not try to exhibit one's insignificant opulence before a greater power.

TEXT 46

तावत् सर्वे वत्सपालाः पश्यतोऽजस्य तत्क्षणात् ।
व्यदृश्यन्त घनश्यामाः पीतकौशेयवाससः ॥४६॥

tāvat sarve vatsa-pālāḥ
paśyato 'jasya tat-kṣaṇāt
vyadṛśyanta ghana-śyāmāḥ
pīta-kauśeya-vāsasaḥ

tāvat—so long; *sarve*—all; *vatsa-pālāḥ*—both the calves and the boys tending them; *paśyataḥ*—while he was watching; *ajasya*—of Lord Brahmā; *tat-kṣaṇāt*—immediately; *vyadṛśyanta*—were seen; *ghana-śyāmāḥ*—as having a complexion resembling bluish rainclouds; *pīta-kauśeya-vāsasaḥ*—and dressed in yellow silk garments.

TRANSLATION

Then, while Lord Brahmā looked on, all the calves and the boys tending them immediately appeared to have complexions the color of bluish rainclouds and to be dressed in yellow silken garments.

PURPORT

While Brahmā was contemplating, all the calves and cowherd boys immediately transformed into *viṣṇu-mūrtis*, having bluish complexions and wearing yellow garments. Brahmā was contemplating his own power and the immense, unlimited power of Kṛṣṇa, but before he could come to a conclusion, he saw this immediate transformation.

TEXTS 47–48

चतुर्भुजाः शङ्खचक्रगदाराजीवपाणयः ।
किरीटिनः कुण्डलिनो हारिणो वनमालिनः ॥४७॥
श्रीवत्साङ्गददोरत्नकम्बुकङ्कणपाणयः ।
नूपुरैः कटकैर्भाताः कटिसूत्राङ्गुलीयकैः ॥४८॥

catur-bhujāḥ śaṅkha-cakra-
gadā-rājīva-pāṇayaḥ
kirīṭinaḥ kuṇḍalino
hāriṇo vana-mālinaḥ

śrīvatsāṅgada-do-ratna-
kambu-kaṅkaṇa-pāṇayaḥ
nūpuraiḥ kaṭakair bhātāḥ
kaṭi-sūtrāṅgulīyakaiḥ

catuḥ-bhujāḥ—having four arms; *śaṅkha-cakra-gadā-rājīva-pāṇayaḥ*—holding conchshell, disc, club and lotus flower in Their hands; *kirīṭinaḥ*—bearing helmets on Their heads; *kuṇḍalinaḥ*—wearing earrings; *hāriṇaḥ*—wearing pearl necklaces; *vana-mālinaḥ*—wearing garlands of forest flowers; *śrīvatsa-aṅgada-do-ratna-kambu-kaṅkaṇa-pāṇayaḥ*—bearing the emblem of the goddess of fortune on Their chests, armlets on Their arms, the Kaustubha gem on Their necks, which were marked with three lines like a conchshell, and bracelets on Their hands; *nūpuraiḥ*—with ornaments on the feet; *kaṭakaiḥ*—with bangles on Their ankles; *bhātāḥ*—appeared beautiful; *kaṭi-sūtra-aṅgulīyakaiḥ*—with sacred belts around the waist and with rings on the fingers.

TRANSLATION

All those personalities had four arms, holding conchshell, disc, mace and lotus flower in Their hands. They wore helmets on Their heads, earrings on Their ears and garlands of forest flowers around Their necks. On the upper portion of the right side of Their chests was the emblem of the goddess of fortune. Furthermore, They wore armlets on Their arms, the Kaustubha gem around Their necks, which were marked with three lines like a conchshell, and bracelets on Their wrists. With bangles on Their ankles, ornaments on Their feet, and sacred belts around Their waists, They all appeared very beautiful.

PURPORT

All the Viṣṇu forms had four arms, with conchshell and other articles, but these characteristics are also possessed by those who have attained *sārūpya-mukti* in Vaikuṇṭha and who consequently have forms exactly like the form of the Lord. However, these Viṣṇu forms appearing before Lord Brahmā also possessed the mark of Śrīvatsa and the Kaustubha gem, which are special characteristics possessed only by the Supreme Lord Himself. This proves that all these boys and calves were in fact directly expansions of Viṣṇu, the Personality of Godhead, not merely His associates of Vaikuṇṭha. Viṣṇu Himself is included within Kṛṣṇa. All the opulences of Viṣṇu are already present in Kṛṣṇa, and consequently for Kṛṣṇa to demonstrate so many Viṣṇu forms was actually not very astonishing.

The Śrīvatsa mark is described by the *Vaiṣṇava-toṣaṇī* as being a curl of fine yellow hair on the upper portion of the right side of Lord Viṣṇu's chest. This mark is not for ordinary devotees. It is a special mark of Viṣṇu or Kṛṣṇa.

TEXT 49

आङ्घ्रिमस्तकमापूर्णास्तुलसीनवदामभिः ।
कोमलैः सर्वगात्रेषु भूरिपुण्यवदर्पितैः ॥४९॥

āṅghri-mastakam āpūrṇās
tulasī-nava-dāmabhiḥ
komalaiḥ sarva-gātreṣu
bhūri-puṇyavad-arpitaiḥ

ā-aṅghri-mastakam—from the feet up to the top of the head; *āpūrṇāḥ*—fully decorated; *tulasī-nava-dāmabhiḥ*—with garlands of fresh *tulasī* leaves; *komalaiḥ*—tender, soft; *sarva-gātreṣu*—on all the limbs of the body; *bhūri-puṇyavat-arpitaiḥ*—which were offered by devotees engaged in the greatest pious activity, worshiping the Supreme Lord by hearing, chanting and so on.

TRANSLATION

Every part of Their bodies, from Their feet to the top of Their heads, was fully decorated with fresh, tender garlands of tulasī leaves offered by devotees engaged in worshiping the Lord by the greatest pious activities, namely hearing and chanting.

PURPORT

The word *bhūri-puṇyavad-arpitaiḥ* is significant in this verse. These forms of Viṣṇu were worshiped by those who had performed pious activities (*sukṛtibhiḥ*) for many births and who were constantly engaged in devotional service (*śravaṇaṁ kīrtanaṁ viṣṇoḥ*). *Bhakti*, devotional service, is the engagement of those who have performed highly developed pious activities. The accumulation of pious activities has already been mentioned elsewhere in the *Śrīmad-Bhāgavatam* (10.12.11), where Śukadeva Gosvāmī says,

itthaṁ satāṁ brahma-sukhānubhūtyā
dāsyaṁ gatānāṁ para-daivatena
māyāśritānāṁ nara-dārakeṇa
sākaṁ vijahruḥ kṛta-puṇya-puñjāḥ

"Those who are engaged in self-realization, appreciating the Brahman effulgence of the Lord, and those engaged in devotional service, accepting the Supreme Personality of Godhead as master, as well as those who are under the clutches of *māyā*, thinking the Lord an ordinary person, cannot understand that certain exalted personalities—after accumulating volumes of pious activities—are now playing with the Lord in friendship as cowherd boys."

In our Kṛṣṇa-Balarāma Temple in Vṛndāvana, there is a *tamāla* tree that covers an entire corner of the courtyard. Before there was a temple the tree was lying neglected, but now it has developed very luxuriantly, covering the whole corner of the courtyard. This is a sign of *bhūri-puṇya.*

TEXT 50

चन्द्रिकाविशदस्मेरैः सारुणापाङ्गवीक्षितैः ।
स्वकार्थानामिव रजःसत्त्वाभ्यां स्रष्टृपालकाः ॥५०॥

candrikā-viśada-smeraiḥ
sāruṇāpāṅga-vīkṣitaiḥ
svakārthānām iva rajaḥ-
sattvābhyāṁ sraṣṭṛ-pālakāḥ

candrikā-viśada-smeraiḥ—by pure smiling like the full, increasing moonlight; *sa-aruṇa-apāṅga-vīkṣitaiḥ*—by the clear glances of Their reddish eyes; *svaka-arthānām*—of the desires of His own devotees; *iva*—just as; *rajaḥ-sattvābhyām*—by the modes of passion and goodness; *sraṣṭṛ-pālakāḥ*—were creators and protectors.

TRANSLATION

Those Viṣṇu forms, by Their pure smiling, which resembled the increasing light of the moon, and by the sidelong glances of Their reddish eyes, created and protected the desires of Their own devotees, as if by the modes of passion and goodness.

PURPORT

Those Viṣṇu forms blessed the devotees with Their clear glances and smiles, which resembled the increasingly full light of the moon (*śreyaḥ-kairava-candrikā-vitaraṇam*). As maintainers, They glanced upon Their devotees, embracing them and protecting them by smiling. Their smiles resembled the mode of goodness, protecting all the desires of the devotees, and the glancing of Their eyes resembled the mode of passion. Actually, in this verse the word *rajaḥ* means not "passion" but "affection." In the material world, *rajo-guṇa* is passion, but in the spiritual world it is affection. In the material world, affection is contaminated by *rajo-guṇa* and *tamo-guṇa*, but in the *śuddha-sattva* the affection that maintains the devotees is transcendental.

The word *svakārthānām* refers to great desires. As mentioned in this verse, the glance of Lord Viṣṇu creates the desires of the devotees. A pure devotee, however, has no desires. Therefore Sanātana Gosvāmī comments that because the desires of devotees whose attention is fixed on Kṛṣṇa have already been fulfilled, the Lord's sidelong glances create variegated desires in relation to Kṛṣṇa and devotional service. In the material world, desire is a product of *rajo-guṇa* and *tamo-guṇa*, but desire in the spiritual world gives rise to a variety of everlasting transcendental service. Thus the word *svakārthānām* refers to eagerness to serve Kṛṣṇa.

In Vṛndāvana there is a place where there was no temple, but a devotee desired, "Let there be a temple and *sevā*, devotional service." Therefore, what was once an empty corner has now become a place of pilgrimage. Such are the desires of a devotee.

TEXT 51

आत्मादिस्तम्बपर्यन्तैर्मूर्तिमद्भिश्चराचरैः ।
नृत्यगीताद्यनेकार्हैः पृथक् पृथगुपासिताः ॥५१॥

ātmādi-stamba-paryantair
mūrtimadbhiś carācaraiḥ
nṛtya-gītādy-anekārhaiḥ
pṛthak pṛthag upāsitāḥ

ātma-ādi-stamba-paryantaiḥ—from Lord Brahmā to the insignificant living entity; *mūrti-madbhiḥ*—assuming some form; *cara-acaraiḥ*—both the moving and the nonmoving; *nṛtya-gīta-ādi-aneka-arhaiḥ*—by many varied means of worship, such as dancing and singing; *pṛthak pṛthak*—differently; *upāsitāḥ*—who were being worshiped.

TRANSLATION

All beings, both moving and nonmoving, from the four-headed Lord Brahmā down to the most insignificant living entity, had taken forms and were differently worshiping those viṣṇu-mūrtis, according to their respective capacities, with various means of worship, such as dancing and singing.

PURPORT

Innumerable living entities are engaged in different types of worship of the Supreme, according to their abilities and *karma*, but everyone is engaged (*jīvera 'svarūpa' haya—kṛṣṇera 'nitya-dāsa'*); there is no one who is not serving. Therefore the *mahā-bhāgavata*, the topmost devotee, sees everyone as being engaged in the service of Kṛṣṇa; only himself does he see as not engaged. We have to elevate ourselves from a lower position to a higher position, and the topmost position is that of direct service in Vṛndāvana. But everyone is engaged in service. Denial of the service of the Lord is *māyā*.

ekale īśvara kṛṣṇa, āra saba bhṛtya
yāre yaiche nācāya, se taiche kare nṛtya

"Only Kṛṣṇa is the supreme master, and all others are His servants. As Kṛṣṇa desires, everyone dances according to His tune." (Cc. *Ādi* 5.142)

There are two kinds of living entities—the moving and the nonmoving. Trees, for example, stand in one place, whereas ants move. Brahmā saw that all of them, down to the smallest creatures, had assumed different forms and were accordingly engaged in the service of Lord Viṣṇu.

One receives a form according to the way one worships the Lord. In the material world, the body one receives is guided by the demigods. This is sometimes referred to as the influence of the stars. As indicated in *Bhagavad-gītā* (3.27) by the words *prakṛteḥ kriyamāṇāni*, according to the laws of nature one is controlled by the demigods.

All living entities are serving Kṛṣṇa in different ways, but when they are Kṛṣṇa conscious, their service is fully manifest. As a flower in the bud gradually fructifies and yields its desired aroma and beauty, so when a living entity comes to the platform of Kṛṣṇa consciousness, the beauty of his real form comes into full blossom. That is the ultimate beauty and the ultimate fulfillment of desire.

TEXT 52

अणिमाद्यैर्महिमभिरजाद्याभिर्विभूतिभिः ।
चतुर्विंशतिभिस्तत्त्वैः परीता महदादिभिः ॥५२॥

aṇimādyair mahimabhir
ajādyābhir vibhūtibhiḥ
catur-viṁśatibhis tattvaiḥ
parītā mahad-ādibhiḥ

aṇimā-ādyaiḥ—headed by *aṇimā; mahimabhiḥ*—by opulences; *ajā-ādyābhiḥ*—headed by Ajā; *vibhūtibhiḥ*—by potencies; *catuḥ-viṁśatibhiḥ*—twenty-four in number; *tattvaiḥ*—by elements for the creation of the material world; *parītāḥ*—(all the *viṣṇu-mūrtis*) were surrounded; *mahat-ādibhiḥ*—headed by the *mahat-tattva.*

TRANSLATION

All the viṣṇu-mūrtis were surrounded by the opulences, headed by aṇimā-siddhi; by the mystic potencies, headed by Ajā; and by

the twenty-four elements for the creation of the material world, headed by the mahat-tattva.

PURPORT

In this verse the word *mahimabhiḥ* means *aiśvarya*, or opulence. The Supreme Personality of Godhead can do whatever He likes. That is His *aiśvarya*. No one can command Him, but He can command everyone. *Ṣaḍ-aiśvarya-pūrṇam.* The Lord is full in six opulences. The *yoga-siddhis*, the perfections of *yoga*, such as the ability to become smaller than the smallest (*aṇimā-siddhi*) or bigger than the biggest (*mahimā-siddhi*), are present in Lord Viṣṇu. *Ṣaḍ-aiśvaryaiḥ pūrṇo ya iha bhagavān* (Cc. *Ādi* 1.3). The word *ajā* means *māyā*, or mystic power. Everything mysterious is in full existence in Viṣṇu.

The twenty-four elements mentioned are the five working senses (*pañca-karmendriya*), the five senses for obtaining knowledge (*pañca-jñānendriya*), the five gross material elements (*pañca-mahābhūta*), the five sense objects (*pañca-tanmātra*), the mind (*manas*), the false ego (*ahaṅkāra*), the *mahat-tattva*, and material nature (*prakṛti*). All twenty-four of these elements are employed for the manifestation of this material world. The *mahat-tattva* is divided into different subtle categories, but originally it is called the *mahat-tattva*.

TEXT 53

कालस्वभावसंस्कारकामकर्मगुणादिभिः ।
स्वमहिध्वस्तमहिभिर्मूर्तिमद्भिरुपासिताः ॥५३॥

kāla-svabhāva-saṁskāra-
kāma-karma-guṇādibhiḥ
sva-mahi-dhvasta-mahibhir
mūrtimadbhir upāsitāḥ

kāla—by the time factor; *svabhāva*—own nature; *saṁskāra*—reformation; *kāma*—desire; *karma*—fruitive action; *guṇa*—the three modes of material nature; *ādibhiḥ*—and by others; *sva-mahi-dhvasta-mahibhiḥ*—whose own independence was subordinate to the potency of the Lord; *mūrti-madbhiḥ*—possessing form; *upāsitāḥ*—were being worshiped.

TRANSLATION

Then Lord Brahmā saw that kāla (the time factor), svabhāva (one's own nature by association), saṁskāra (reformation), kāma (desire), karma (fruitive activity) and the guṇas (the three modes of material nature), their own independence being completely subordinate to the potency of the Lord, had all taken forms and were also worshiping those viṣṇu-mūrtis.

PURPORT

No one but Viṣṇu has any independence. If we develop consciousness of this fact, then we are in actual Kṛṣṇa consciousness. We should always remember that Kṛṣṇa is the only supreme master and that everyone else is His servant (*ekale īśvara kṛṣṇa, āra saba bhṛtya*). Be one even Nārāyaṇa or Lord Śiva, everyone is subordinate to Kṛṣṇa (*śiva-viriñci-nutam*). Even Baladeva is subordinate to Kṛṣṇa. This is a fact.

ekale īśvara kṛṣṇa, āra saba bhṛtya
yāre yaiche nācāya, se taiche kare nṛtya
(Cc. *Ādi* 5.142)

One should understand that no one is independent, for everything is part and parcel of Kṛṣṇa and is acting and moving by the supreme desire of Kṛṣṇa. This understanding, this consciousness, is Kṛṣṇa consciousness.

yas tu nārāyaṇaṁ devaṁ
brahma-rudrādi-daivataiḥ
samatvenaiva vīkṣeta
sa pāṣaṇḍī bhaved dhruvam

"A person who considers demigods like Brahmā and Śiva to be on an equal level with Nārāyaṇa must certainly be considered an offender." No one can compare to Nārāyaṇa, or Kṛṣṇa. Kṛṣṇa is Nārāyaṇa, and Nārāyaṇa is also Kṛṣṇa, for Kṛṣṇa is the original Nārāyaṇa. Brahmā himself addresses Kṛṣṇa, *nārāyaṇas tvaṁ na hi sarva-dehinām:* "You are also Nārāyaṇa. Indeed, You are the original Nārāyaṇa." (*Bhāg.* 10.14.14)

Kāla, or the time factor, has many assistants, such as *svabhāva, saṁskāra, kāma, karma* and *guṇa. Svabhāva,* or one's own nature, is formed according to the association of the material qualities. *Kāraṇaṁ guṇa-saṅgo 'sya sad-asad-yoni-janmasu* (Bg. 13.22). *Sat* and *asat-svabhāva*—one's higher or lower nature—is formed by association with the different qualities, namely *sattva-guṇa*, *rajo-guṇa* and *tamo-guṇa*. We should gradually come to the *sattva-guṇa*, so that we may avoid the two lower *guṇas*. This can be done if we regularly discuss *Śrīmad-Bhāgavatam* and hear about Kṛṣṇa's activities. *Naṣṭa-prāyeṣv abhadreṣu nityaṁ bhāgavata-sevayā* (*Bhāg.* 1.2.18). All the activities of Kṛṣṇa described in *Śrīmad-Bhāgavatam*, beginning even with the pastimes concerning Pūtanā, are transcendental. Therefore, by hearing and discussing *Śrīmad-Bhāgavatam*, the *rajo-guṇa* and *tamo-guṇa* are subdued, so that only *sattva-guṇa* remains. Then *rajo-guṇa* and *tamo-guṇa* cannot do us any harm.

Varṇāśrama-dharma, therefore, is essential, for it can bring people to *sattva-guṇa*. *Tadā rajas-tamo-bhāvāḥ kāma-lobhādayaś ca ye* (*Bhāg.* 1.2.19). *Tamo-guṇa* and *rajo-guṇa* increase lust and greed, which implicate a living entity in such a way that he must exist in this material world in many, many forms. That is very dangerous. One should therefore be brought to *sattva-guṇa* by the establishment of *varṇāśrama-dharma* and should develop the brahminical qualifications of being very neat and clean, rising early in the morning and seeing *maṅgala-ārātrika*, and so on. In this way, one should stay in *sattva-guṇa*, and then one cannot be influenced by *tamo-guṇa* and *rajo-guṇa*.

tadā rajas-tamo-bhāvāḥ
kāma-lobhādayaś ca ye
ceta etair anāviddhaṁ
sthitaṁ sattve prasīdati
(*Bhāg.* 1.2.19)

The opportunity for this purification is the special feature of human life; in other lives, this is not possible. Such purification can be achieved very easily by *rādhā-kṛṣṇa-bhajana*, devotional service rendered to Rādhā and Kṛṣṇa, and therefore Narottama dāsa Ṭhākura sings, *hari hari viphale janama goṅāinu*, indicating that unless one worships Rādhā-Kṛṣṇa, one's human form of life is wasted. *Vāsudeve bhagavati bhakti-yogaḥ prayojitaḥ/ janayaty āśu vairāgyam* (*Bhāg.* 1.2.7). By engagement in the service of Vāsudeva, one very quickly renounces material life. The members of the Kṛṣṇa consciousness movement, for example, being engaged in *vāsudeva-bhakti,* very quickly come to the stage of being nice Vaiṣṇavas, so much so that people are surprised that *mlecchas* and *yavanas* are able to come to this stage. This is possible by *vāsudeva-bhakti.* But if we do not come to the stage of *sattva-guṇa* in this human life, then, as Narottama dāsa Ṭhākura sings, *hari hari viphale janama goṅāinu*—there is no profit in gaining this human form of life.

Śrī Vīrarāghava Ācārya comments that each of the items mentioned in the first half of this verse is a cause for material entanglement. *Kāla,* or the time factor, agitates the modes of material nature, and *svabhāva* is the result of association with these modes. Therefore Narottama dāsa Ṭhākura says, *bhakta-sane vāsa.* If one associates with *bhaktas,* then one's *svabhāva,* or nature, will change. Our Kṛṣṇa consciousness movement is meant to give people good association so that this change may take place, and we actually see that by this method people all over the world are gradually becoming devotees.

As for *saṁskāra,* or reformation, this is possible by good association, for by good association one develops good habits, and habit becomes second nature. Therefore, *bhakta-sane vāsa:* let people have the chance to live with *bhaktas.* Then their habits will change. In the human form of life one has this chance, but as Narottama dāsa Ṭhākura sings, *hari hari viphale janama goṅāinu:* if one fails to take advantage of this opportunity, one's human life is wasted. We are therefore trying to save human society from degradation and actually elevate people to the higher nature.

As for *kāma* and *karma*—desires and activities—if one engages in devotional service, one develops a different nature than if one engages in activities of sense gratification, and of course the result is also different. According to the association of different natures, one receives a particular type of body. *Kāraṇaṁ guṇa-saṅgo 'sya sad-asad-yoni-janmasu* (Bg. 13.22). Therefore we should always seek good association, the association of devotees. Then our life will be successful. A man is known by his company. If one has the chance to live in the good association of devotees, one is able to cultivate knowledge, and naturally one's character or nature will change for one's eternal benefit.

TEXT 54

सत्यज्ञानानन्तानन्दमात्रैकरसमूर्तयः ।
अस्पृष्टभूरिमाहात्म्या अपि ह्युपनिषद्दृशाम् ॥५४॥

satya-jñānānantānanda-
mātraika-rasa-mūrtayaḥ
aspṛṣṭa-bhūri-māhātmyā
api hy upaniṣad-dṛśām

satya—eternal; *jñāna*—having full knowledge; *ananta*—unlimited; *ānanda*—fully blissful; *mātra*—only; *eka-rasa*—always existing; *mūrtayaḥ*—forms; *aspṛṣṭa-bhūri-māhātmyāḥ*—whose great glory is not touched; *api*—even; *hi*—because; *upaniṣat-dṛśām*—by those *jñānīs* who are engaged in studying the *Upaniṣads.*

TRANSLATION

The viṣṇu-mūrtis all had eternal, unlimited forms, full of knowledge and bliss and existing beyond the influence of time. Their great glory was not even to be touched by the jñānīs engaged in studying the Upaniṣads.

PURPORT

Mere *śāstra-jñāna,* or knowledge in the *Vedas,* does not help anyone understand the Personality of Godhead. Only one who is favored or shown mercy by the Lord can understand Him. This is also explained in the *Upaniṣads* (*Muṇḍaka Up.* 3.2.3):

nāyam ātmā pravacanena labhyo
na medhasā na bahunā śrutena
yam evaiṣa vṛṇute tena labhyas
tasyaiṣa ātmā vivṛṇute tanuṁ svām

"The Supreme Lord is not obtained by expert explanations, by vast intelligence, or even by much hearing. He is obtained only by one whom He Himself chooses. To such a person, He manifests His own form."

One description given of Brahman is *satyaṁ brahma, ānanda-rūpam:* "Brahman is the Absolute Truth and complete *ānanda*, or bliss." The forms of Viṣṇu, the Supreme Brahman, were one, but They were manifested differently. The followers of the *Upaniṣads*, however, cannot understand the varieties manifested by Brahman. This proves that Brahman and Paramātmā can actually be understood only through devotion, as confirmed by the Lord Himself in *Śrīmad-Bhāgavatam* (*bhaktyāham ekayā grāhyaḥ, Bhāg.* 11.14.21). To establish that Brahman indeed has transcendental form, Śrīla Viśvanātha Cakravartī Ṭhākura gives various quotations from the *śāstras*. In the *Śvetāśvatara Upaniṣad* (3.8), the Supreme is described as *āditya-varṇaṁ tamasaḥ parastāt*, "He whose self-manifest form is luminous like the sun and transcendental to the darkness of ignorance." *Ānanda-mātram ajaraṁ purāṇam ekaṁ santaṁ bahudhā dṛśyamānam:* "The Supreme is blissful, with no tinge of unhappiness. Although He is the oldest, He never ages, and although one, He is experienced in different forms." *Sarve nityāḥ śāśvatāś ca dehās tasya parātmanaḥ:* "All the forms of that Supreme Person are eternal." (*Mahā-varāha Purāṇa*) The Supreme Person has a form, with hands and legs and other personal features, but His hands and legs are not material. *Bhaktas* know that the form of Kṛṣṇa, or Brahman, is not at all material. Rather, Brahman has a transcendental form, and when one is absorbed in it, being fully developed in *bhakti*, one can understand Him (*premāñjana-cchurita-bhakti-vilocanena*). The Māyāvādīs, however, cannot understand this transcendental form, for they think that it is material.

Transcendental forms of the Supreme Personality of Godhead in His person are so great that the impersonal followers of the *Upaniṣads* cannot reach the platform of knowledge to understand them. Particularly, the transcendental forms of the Lord are beyond the reach of the impersonalists, who can only understand, through the studies of the *Upaniṣads*, that the Absolute Truth is not matter and that the Absolute Truth is not materially restricted by limited potency.

Yet although Kṛṣṇa cannot be seen through the *Upaniṣads*, in some places it is said that Kṛṣṇa can in fact be known in this way. *Aupaniṣadaṁ puruṣam:* "He is known by the *Upaniṣads*." This means that when one is purified by Vedic knowledge, one is then allowed to enter into devotional understanding (*mad-bhaktiṁ labhate parām*).

tac chraddadhānā munayo
jñāna-vairagya-yuktayā
paśyanty ātmani cātmānaṁ
bhaktyā śruta-gṛhītayā

"The seriously inquisitive student or sage, well equipped with knowledge and detachment, realizes that Absolute Truth by rendering devotional service in terms of what he has heard from the *Vedānta-śruti.*" (*Bhāg.* 1.2.12) The word *śruta-gṛhītayā* refers to *Vedānta* knowledge, not sentimentality. *Śruta-gṛhīta* is sound knowledge.

Lord Viṣṇu, Brahmā thus realized, is the reservoir of all truth, knowledge and bliss. He is the combination of these three transcendental features, and He is the object of worship for the followers of the *Upaniṣads.* Brahmā realized that all the different forms of cows, boys and calves transformed into Viṣṇu forms were not transformed by mysticism of the type that a *yogī* or demigod can display by specific powers invested in him. The cows, calves and boys transformed into *viṣṇu-mūrtis,* or Viṣṇu forms, were not displays of *viṣṇu-māyā,* or Viṣṇu energy, but were Viṣṇu Himself. The respective qualifications of Viṣṇu and *viṣṇu-māyā* are just like those of fire and heat. In heat there is the qualification of fire, namely warmth; and yet heat is not fire. The manifestation of the Viṣṇu forms of the boys, cows and calves was not like the heat, but rather like the fire—they were all actually Viṣṇu. Factually, the qualification of Viṣṇu is full truth, full knowledge and full bliss. Another example may be given with material objects, which may be reflected in many, many forms. For example, the sun is reflected in many waterpots, but the reflections of the sun in many pots are not actually the sun. There is no actual heat and light from the sun in the pot, although it appears as the sun. But each and every one of the forms Kṛṣṇa assumed was fully Viṣṇu.

We should discuss *Śrīmad-Bhāgavatam* daily as much as possible, and then everything will be clarified, for *Bhāgavatam* is the essence of all Vedic literature (*nigama-kalpataror galitaṁ phalam*). It was written by Vyāsadeva (*mahāmuni-kṛte*) when he was self-realized. Thus the more we read *Śrīmad-Bhāgavatam,* the more its knowledge becomes clear. Each and every verse is transcendental.

TEXT 55

एवं सकृद् ददर्शाजः परब्रह्मात्मनोऽखिलान् ।
यस्य भासा सर्वमिदं विभाति सचराचरम् ॥५५॥

evaṁ sakṛd dadarśājaḥ
para-brahmātmano 'khilān
yasya bhāsā sarvam idaṁ
vibhāti sa-carācaram

evam—thus; *sakṛt*—at one time; *dadarśa*—saw; *ajaḥ*—Lord Brahmā; *para-brahma*—of the Supreme Absolute Truth; *ātmanaḥ*—expansions; *akhilān*—all the calves and boys, etc.; *yasya*—of whom; *bhāsā*—by the manifestation; *sarvam*—all; *idam*—this; *vibhāti*—is manifested; *sa-cara-acaram*—whatever is moving and nonmoving.

TRANSLATION

Thus Lord Brahmā saw the Supreme Brahman, by whose energy this entire universe, with its moving and nonmoving living beings, is manifested. He also saw at the same time all the calves and boys as the Lord's expansions.

PURPORT

By this incident, Lord Brahmā was able to see how Kṛṣṇa maintains the entire universe in different ways. It is because Kṛṣṇa manifests everything that everything is visible.

TEXT 56

ततोऽतिकुतुकोद्वृत्यस्तिमितैकादशेन्द्रियः ।
तद्धाम्नाभूदजस्तूष्णीं पूर्देव्यन्तीव पुत्रिका ॥५६॥

tato 'tikutukodvṛtya-
stimitaikādaśendriyaḥ
tad-dhāmnābhūd ajas tūṣṇīṁ
pūr-devy-antīva putrikā

tataḥ—then; *atikutuka-udvṛtya-stimita-ekādaśa-indriyaḥ*—whose eleven senses had all been jolted by great astonishment and then stunned by transcendental bliss; *tad-dhāmnā*—by the effulgence of those *viṣṇu-mūrtis; abhūt*—became; *ajaḥ*—Lord Brahmā; *tūṣṇīm*—silent; *pūḥ-devī-anti*—in the presence of a village deity (*grāmya-devatā*); *iva*—just as; *putrikā*—a clay doll made by a child.

TRANSLATION

Then, by the power of the effulgence of those viṣṇu-mūrtis, Lord Brahmā, his eleven senses jolted by astonishment and stunned by transcendental bliss, became silent, just like a child's clay doll in the presence of the village deity.

PURPORT

Brahmā was stunned because of transcendental bliss (*muhyanti yat sūrayaḥ*). In his astonishment, all his senses were stunned, and he was unable to say or do anything. Brahmā had considered himself absolute, thinking himself the only powerful deity, but now his pride was subdued, and he again became merely one of the demigods—an important demigod, of course, but a demigod nonetheless. Brahmā, therefore, cannot be compared to God—Kṛṣṇa, or Nārāyaṇa. It is forbidden to compare Nārāyaṇa even to demigods like Brahmā and Śiva, what to speak of others.

yas tu nārāyaṇaṁ devaṁ
brahma-rudrādi-daivataiḥ
samatvenaiva vīkṣeta
sa pāṣaṇḍī bhaved dhruvam

"One who considers demigods like Brahmā and Śiva to be on an equal level with Nārāyaṇa must certainly be considered an offender." We should not equate the demigods with Nārāyaṇa, for even Śaṅkarācārya has forbidden this (*nārāyaṇaḥ paro 'vyaktāt*). Also, as mentioned in the *Vedas*, *eko nārāyaṇa āsīn na brahmā neśānaḥ:* "In the beginning of creation there was only the Supreme Personality, Nārāyaṇa, and there was no existence of Brahmā or Śiva." Therefore, one who at the end of his life remembers Nārāyaṇa attains the perfection of life (*ante nārāyaṇa-smṛtiḥ*).

TEXT 57

इतीरेशेऽतर्क्ये निजमहिमनि स्वप्रमितिके
परत्राजातोऽतन्निरसनमुखब्रह्मकमितौ ।
अनीशेऽपि द्रष्टुं किमिदमिति वा मुह्यति सति
चच्छादाजो ज्ञात्वा सपदि परमोऽजाजवनिकाम् ॥५७॥

itīreśe 'tarkye nija-mahimani sva-pramitike
paratrājāto 'tan-nirasana-mukha-brahmaka-mitau
anīśe 'pi draṣṭuṁ kim idam iti vā muhyati sati
cacchādājo jñātvā sapadi paramo 'jā-javanikām

iti—thus; *irā-īśe*—Lord Brahmā, the lord of Sarasvatī (Irā); *atarkye*—beyond; *nija-mahimani*—whose own glory; *sva-pramitike*—self-manifest and blissful; *paratra*—beyond; *ajātaḥ*—the material energy (*prakṛti*); *atat*—irrelevant; *nirasana-mukha*—by the rejection of that which is irrelevant; *brahmaka*—by the crest jewels of the *Vedas; mitau*—in whom there is knowledge; *anīśe*—not being able; *api*—even; *draṣṭum*—to see; *kim*—what; *idam*—is this; *iti*—thus; *vā*—or; *muhyati sati*—being mystified; *cacchāda*—removed; *ajaḥ*—Lord Śrī Kṛṣṇa; *jñātvā*—after understanding; *sapadi*—at once; *paramaḥ*—the greatest of all; *ajā-javanikām*—the curtain of *māyā.*

TRANSLATION

The Supreme Brahman is beyond mental speculation, He is self-manifest, existing in His own bliss, and He is beyond the material energy. He is known by the crest jewels of the Vedas by refutation of irrelevant knowledge. Thus in relation to that Supreme Brahman, the Personality of Godhead, whose glory had been shown by the manifestation of all the four-armed forms of Viṣṇu, Lord Brahmā, the lord of Sarasvatī, was mystified. "What is this?" he thought, and then he was not even able to see. Lord Kṛṣṇa, understanding Brahmā's position, then at once removed the curtain of His yogamāyā.

PURPORT

Brahmā was completely mystified. He could not understand what he was seeing, and then he was not even able to see. Lord Kṛṣṇa, understanding Brahmā's position, then removed that *yogamāyā* covering. In this verse, Brahmā is referred to as *ireśa. Irā* means Sarasvatī, the goddess of learning, and Ireśa is her husband, Lord Brahmā. Brahmā, therefore, is most intelligent. But even Brahmā, the lord of Sarasvatī, was bewildered about Kṛṣṇa. Although he tried, he could not understand Lord Kṛṣṇa. In the beginning the boys, the calves and Kṛṣṇa Himself had been covered by *yogamāyā,* which later displayed the second set of calves and boys, who were Kṛṣṇa's expansions, and which then displayed so many four-armed forms. Now, seeing Brahmā's bewilderment, Lord Kṛṣṇa caused the disappearance of that *yogamāyā.* One may think that the *māyā* taken away by Lord Kṛṣṇa was *mahāmāyā,* but Śrīla Viśvanātha Cakravartī Ṭhākura comments that it was *yogamāyā,* the potency by which Kṛṣṇa is sometimes manifest and sometimes not manifest. The potency which covers the actual reality and displays something unreal is *mahāmāyā,* but the potency by which the Absolute Truth is sometimes manifest and sometimes not is *yogamāyā.* Therefore, in this verse the word *ajā* refers to *yogamāyā.*

Kṛṣṇa's energy—His *māyā-śakti,* or *svarūpa-śakti*—is one, but it is manifested in varieties. *Parāsya śaktir vividhaiva śrūyate* (*Śvetāśvatara Up.* 6.8). The difference between Vaiṣṇavas and Māyāvādīs is that Māyāvādīs say that this *māyā* is one, whereas Vaiṣṇavas recognize its varieties. There is unity in variety. For example, in one tree, there are varieties of leaves, fruits and flowers. Varieties of energy are required for performing the varieties of activity within the creation. To give another example, in a machine all the parts may be iron, but the machine includes varied activities. Although the whole machine is iron, one part works in one way, and other parts work in other ways. One who does not know how the machine is working may say that it is all iron; nonetheless, in spite of its being iron, the machine has different elements, all working differently to accomplish the purpose for which the machine was made. One wheel runs this way, another wheel runs that way, functioning naturally in such a way that the work of the machine goes on. Consequently we give different names to the different parts of the machine, saying, "This is a wheel," "This is a screw," "This is a spindle," "This is the lubrication," and so on. Similarly, as explained in the *Vedas,*

parāsya śaktir vividhaiva śrūyate
svābhāvikī jñāna-bala-kriyā ca

Kṛṣṇa's power is variegated, and thus the same *śakti,* or potency, works in variegated ways. *Vividhā* means "varieties." There is unity in variety. Thus *yogamāyā* and *mahāmāyā* are among the varied individual parts of the same one potency, and all of these individual potencies work in their own varied ways. The *saṁvit, sandhinī* and *āhlādinī* potencies—Kṛṣṇa's potency for existence, His potency for knowledge and His potency for pleasure—are distinct from *yogamāyā.* Each is an individual potency. The *āhlādinī* potency is Rādhārāṇī. As Svarūpa Dāmodara Gosvāmī has explained, *rādhā kṛṣṇa-praṇaya-vikṛtir hlādinī śaktir asmāt* (Cc. *Ādi* 1.5). The *āhlādinī-śakti* is manifested as Rādhārāṇī, but Kṛṣṇa and Rādhārāṇī are the same, although one is potent and the other is potency.

Brahmā was mystified about Kṛṣṇa's opulence (*nija-mahimani*) because this opulence was *atarkya,* or inconceivable. With one's limited senses, one cannot argue about that which is inconceivable. Therefore the inconceivable is called *acintya,* that which is beyond *cintya,* our thoughts and arguments. *Acintya* refers to that which we cannot contemplate but have to accept. Śrīla Jīva Gosvāmī has said that unless we accept *acintya* in the Supreme, we cannot accommodate the conception of God. This must be understood. Therefore we say that the words of *śāstra* should be taken as they are, without change, since they are beyond our arguments. *Acintyāḥ khalu ye bhāvā na tāṁs tarkeṇa yojayet:* "That which is *acintya* cannot be ascertained by argument." People generally argue, but our process is not to argue but to accept the Vedic knowledge as it is. When Kṛṣṇa says, "This is superior, and this is inferior," we accept what He says. It is not that we argue, "Why is this superior and that inferior?" If one argues, for him the knowledge is lost.

This path of acceptance is called *avaroha-panthā.* The word *avaroha* is related to the word *avatāra,* which means "that which descends." The materialist wants to understand everything by the *āroha-panthā*—by argument and reason—but transcendental matters cannot be understood in this way. Rather, one must follow the *avaroha-panthā,* the process of descending knowledge. Therefore one must accept the *paramparā* system. And the best *paramparā* is that which extends from Kṛṣṇa (*evaṁ paramparā-prāptam*). What Kṛṣṇa says, we should accept (*imaṁ rājarṣayo viduḥ*). This is called the *avaroha-panthā.*

Brahmā, however, adopted the *āroha-panthā.* He wanted to understand Kṛṣṇa's mystic power by his own limited, conceivable power, and therefore he himself was mystified. Everyone wants to take pleasure in his own knowledge, thinking, "I know something." But in the presence of Kṛṣṇa this conception cannot stand, for one cannot bring Kṛṣṇa within the limitations of *prakṛti.* One must submit. There is no alternative. *Na tāṁs tarkeṇa yojayet.* This submission marks the difference between Kṛṣṇa-ites and Māyāvādīs.

The phrase *atan-nirasana* refers to the discarding of that which is irrelevant. (*Atat* means "that which is not a fact.") Brahman is sometimes described as *asthūlam anaṇv ahrasvam adīrgham,* "that which is not large and not small, not short and not long." (*Bṛhad-āraṇyaka Up.* 5.8.8) *Neti neti:* "It is not this, it is not that." But what is it? In describing a pencil, one may say, "It is not this; it is not that," but this does not tell us what it is. This is called definition by negation. In *Bhagavad-gītā,* Kṛṣṇa also explains the soul by giving negative definitions. *Na jāyate mriyate vā:* "It is not born, nor does it die. You can hardly understand more than this." But what is it? It is eternal. *Ajo nityaḥ śāśvato 'yaṁ purāṇo na hanyate hanyamāne śarīre:* "It is unborn, eternal, ever-existing, undying and primeval. It is not slain when the body is slain." (Bg. 2.20) In the beginning the soul is difficult to understand, and therefore Kṛṣṇa has given negative definitions:

nainaṁ chindanti śastrāṇi
nainaṁ dahati pāvakaḥ
na cainaṁ kledayanty āpo
na śoṣayati mārutaḥ

"The soul can never be cut into pieces by any weapon, nor can it be burned by fire, nor moistened by water, nor withered by the wind." (Bg. 2.23) Kṛṣṇa says, "It is not burned by fire." Therefore, one has to imagine what it is that is not burned by fire. This is a negative definition.

TEXT 58

ततोऽर्वाक् प्रतिलब्धाक्षः कः परेतवदुत्थितः ।
कृच्छ्रादुन्मील्य वै दृष्टीराचष्टेदं सहात्मना ॥५८॥

tato 'rvāk pratilabdhākṣaḥ
kaḥ paretavad utthitaḥ
kṛcchrād unmīlya vai dṛṣṭīr
ācaṣṭedaṁ sahātmanā

tataḥ—then; *arvāk*—externally; *pratilabdha-akṣaḥ*—having revived his consciousness; *kaḥ*—Lord Brahmā; *pareta-vat*—just like a dead man; *utthitaḥ*—stood up; *kṛcchrāt*—with great difficulty; *unmīlya*—opening up; *vai*—indeed; *dṛṣṭīḥ*—his eyes; *ācaṣṭa*—he saw; *idam*—this universe; *saha-ātmanā*—along with himself.

TRANSLATION

Lord Brahmā's external consciousness then revived, and he stood up, just like a dead man coming back to life. Opening his eyes with great difficulty, he saw the universe, along with himself.

PURPORT

We actually do not die. At death, we are merely kept inert for some time, just as during sleep. At night we sleep, and all our activities stop, but as soon as we arise, our memory immediately returns, and we think, "Oh, where am I? What do I have to do?" This is called *suptotthita-nyāya.* Suppose we die. "Die" means that we become inert for some time and then again begin our activities. This takes place life after life, according to our *karma,* or activities, and *svabhāva,* or nature by association. Now, in the human life, if we prepare ourselves by beginning the activity of our spiritual life, we return to our real life and attain perfection. Otherwise, according to *karma, svabhāva, prakṛti* and so on, our varieties of life and activity continue, and so also do our birth and death. As explained by Bhaktivinoda Ṭhākura, *māyāra vaśe, yāccha bhese, khāccha hābuḍubu bhāi:* "My dear brothers, why are you being washed away by the waves of *māyā*?" One should come to the spiritual platform, and then one's activities will be permanent. *Kṛta-puṇya-puñjāḥ:* this stage is attained after one accumulates the results of pious activities for many, many lives. *Janma-koṭi-sukṛtair na labhyate* (Cc. *Madhya* 8.70). The Kṛṣṇa consciousness movement wants to stop *koṭi-janma,* repeated birth and death. In one birth, one should rectify everything and come to permanent life. This is Kṛṣṇa consciousness.

TEXT 59

सपद्येवाभितः पश्यन् दिशोऽपश्यत् पुरःस्थितम् ।
वृन्दावनं जनाजीव्यद्रुमाकीर्णं समाप्रियम् ॥५९॥

sapady evābhitaḥ paśyan
diśo 'paśyat puraḥ-sthitam
vṛndāvanaṁ janājīvya-
drumākīrṇaṁ samā-priyam

sapadi—immediately; *eva*—indeed; *abhitaḥ*—on all sides; *paśyan*—looking; *diśaḥ*—in the directions; *apaśyat*—Lord Brahmā saw; *puraḥ-sthitam*—situated in front of him; *vṛndāvanam*—Vṛndāvana; *jana-ājīvya-druma-ākīrṇam*—dense with trees, which were the means of living for the inhabitants; *samā-priyam*—and which was equally pleasing in all seasons.

TRANSLATION

Then, looking in all directions, Lord Brahmā immediately saw Vṛndāvana before him, filled with trees, which were the means of livelihood for the inhabitants and which were equally pleasing in all seasons.

PURPORT

Janājīvya-drumākīrṇam: trees and vegetables are essential, and they give happiness all year round, in all seasons. That is the arrangement in Vṛndāvana. It is not that in one season the trees are pleasing and in another season not pleasing; rather, they are equally pleasing throughout the seasonal changes. Trees and vegetables provide the real means of livelihood recommended for everyone. *Sarva-kāma-dughā mahī* (*Bhāg.* 1.10.4). Trees and vegetables, not industry, provide the real means of life.

TEXT 60

यत्र नैसर्गदुर्वैराः सहासन् नृमृगादयः ।
मित्राणीवाजितावासद्रुतरुट्तर्षकादिकम् ॥६०॥

yatra naisarga-durvairāḥ
sahāsan nṛ-mṛgādayaḥ
mitrāṇīvājitāvāsa-
druta-ruṭ-tarṣakādikam

yatra—where; *naisarga*—by nature; *durvairāḥ*—living in enmity; *saha āsan*—live together; *nṛ*—human beings; *mṛga-ādayaḥ*—and animals; *mitrāṇi*—friends; *iva*—like; *ajita*—of Lord Śrī Kṛṣṇa; *āvāsa*—residence; *druta*—gone away; *ruṭ*—anger; *tarṣaka-ādikam*—thirst and so on.

TRANSLATION

Vṛndāvana is the transcendental abode of the Lord, where there is no hunger, anger or thirst. Though naturally inimical, both human beings and fierce animals live there together in transcendental friendship.

PURPORT

The word *vana* means "forest." We are afraid of the forest and do not wish to go there, but in Vṛndāvana the forest animals are as good as demigods, for they have no envy. Even in this material world, in the forest the animals live together, and when they go to drink water they do not attack anyone. Envy develops because of sense gratification, but in Vṛndāvana there is no sense gratification, for the only aim is Kṛṣṇa's satisfaction. Even in this material world, the animals in Vṛndāvana are not envious of the *sādhus* who live there. The *sādhus* keep cows and supply milk to the tigers, saying, "Come here and take a little milk." Thus envy and malice are unknown in Vṛndāvana. That is the difference between Vṛndāvana and the ordinary world. We are horrified to hear the name of *vana,* the forest, but in Vṛndāvana there is no such horror. Everyone there is happy by pleasing Kṛṣṇa. *Kṛṣṇotkīrtana-gāna-nartana-parau.* Whether a *gosvāmī* or a tiger or other ferocious animal, everyone's business is the same—to please Kṛṣṇa. Even the tigers are also devotees. This is the specific qualification of Vṛndāvana. In Vṛndāvana everyone is happy. The calf is happy, the cat is happy, the dog is happy, the man is happy—everyone. Everyone wants to serve Kṛṣṇa in a different capacity, and thus there is no envy. One may sometimes think that the monkeys in Vṛndāvana are envious, because they cause mischief and steal food, but in Vṛndāvana we find that the monkeys are allowed to take butter, which Kṛṣṇa Himself distributes. Kṛṣṇa personally demonstrates that everyone has the right to live. This is Vṛndāvana life. Why should I live and you die? No. That is material life. The inhabitants of Vṛndāvana think, "Whatever is given by Kṛṣṇa, let us divide it as *prasāda* and eat." This mentality cannot appear all of a sudden, but it will gradually develop with Kṛṣṇa consciousness; by *sādhana,* one can come to this platform.

In the material world one may collect funds all over the world in order to distribute food freely, yet those to whom the food is given may not even feel appreciative. The value of Kṛṣṇa consciousness, however, will gradually be very much appreciated. For instance, in an article about the temple of the Hare Kṛṣṇa movement in Durban, South Africa, the *Durban Post* reported, "All the devotees here are very active in the service of Lord Kṛṣṇa, and the results are obvious to see: happiness, good health, peace of mind, and the development of all good qualities." This is the nature of Vṛndāvana. *Harāv abhaktasya kuto mahad-guṇāḥ:* without Kṛṣṇa consciousness, happiness is impossible; one may struggle, but one cannot have happiness. We are therefore trying to give human society the opportunity for a life of happiness, good health, peace of mind and all good qualities through God consciousness.

TEXT 61

तत्रोद्वहत् पशुपवंशशिशुत्वनाट्यं
ब्रह्माद्वयं परमनन्तमगाधबोधम् ।
वत्सान् सखीनिव पुरा परितो विचिन्व-
देकं सपाणिकवलं परमेष्ठ्यचष्ट ॥६१॥

tatrodvahat paśupa-vaṁśa-śiśutva-nāṭyaṁ
brahmādvayaṁ param anantam agādha-bodham
vatsān sakhīn iva purā parito vicinvad
ekaṁ sa-pāṇi-kavalaṁ parameṣṭhy acaṣṭa

tatra—there (in Vṛndāvana); *udvahat*—assuming; *paśupa-vaṁśa-śiśutva-nāṭyam*—the play of being a child in a family of cowherd men (another of Kṛṣṇa's names is Gopāla, "He who maintains the cows"); *brahma*—the Absolute Truth; *advayam*—without a second; *param*—the Supreme; *anantam*—unlimited; *agādha-bodham*—possessing unlimited knowledge; *vatsān*—the calves; *sakhīn*—and His friends, the boys; *iva purā*—just as before; *paritaḥ*—everywhere; *vicinvat*—searching; *ekam*—alone, all by Himself; *sa-pāṇi-kavalam*—with a morsel of food in His hand; *parameṣṭhī*—Lord Brahmā; *acaṣṭa*—saw.

TRANSLATION

Then Lord Brahmā saw the Absolute Truth—who is one without a second, who possesses full knowledge and who is unlimited—assuming the role of a child in a family of cowherd men and standing all alone, just as before, with a morsel of food in His hand, searching everywhere for the calves and His cowherd friends.

PURPORT

The word *agādha-bodham,* meaning "full of unlimited knowledge," is significant in this verse. The Lord's knowledge is unlimited, and therefore one cannot touch where it ends, just as one cannot measure the ocean. What is the extent of our intelligence in comparison to the vast expanse of water in the ocean? On my passage to America, how insignificant the ship was, like a matchbox in the midst of the ocean. Kṛṣṇa's intelligence resembles the ocean, for one cannot imagine how vast it is. The best course, therefore, is to surrender to Kṛṣṇa. Don't try to measure Kṛṣṇa.

The word *advayam,* meaning "one without a second," is also significant. Because Brahmā was overcast by Kṛṣṇa's *māyā,* he was thinking himself the Supreme. In the material world, everyone thinks, "I am the best man in this world. I know everything." One thinks, "Why should I read *Bhagavad-gītā?* I know everything. I have my own interpretation."

Brahmā, however, was able to understand that the Supreme Personality is Kṛṣṇa. *Īśvaraḥ paramaḥ kṛṣṇaḥ.* Another of Kṛṣṇa's names, therefore, is *parameśvara.*

Now Brahmā saw Kṛṣṇa, the Supreme Personality of Godhead, appearing as a cowherd boy in Vṛndāvana, not demonstrating His opulence but standing just like an innocent boy with some food in His hand, loitering with His cowherd boyfriends, calves and cows. Brahmā did not see Kṛṣṇa as *catur-bhuja*, the opulent Nārāyaṇa; rather, he simply saw an innocent boy. Nonetheless, he could understand that although Kṛṣṇa was not demonstrating His power, He was the same Supreme Person. People generally do not appreciate someone unless he shows something wonderful, but here, although Kṛṣṇa did not manifest anything wonderful, Brahmā could understand that the same wonderful person was present like an ordinary child, although He was the master of the whole creation. Thus Brahmā prayed, *govindam ādi-puruṣaṁ tam ahaṁ bhajāmi:* "You are the original person, the cause of everything. I bow down to You." This was his realization. *Tam ahaṁ bhajāmi.* This is what is wanted. *Vedeṣu durlabham:* one cannot reach Kṛṣṇa merely by Vedic knowledge. *Adurlabham ātma-bhaktau:* but when one becomes a devotee, then one can realize Him. Brahmā, therefore, became a devotee. In the beginning he was proud of being Brahmā, the lord of the universe, but now he understood, "Here is the Lord of the universe. I am simply an insignificant agent. *Govindam ādi-puruṣaṁ tam ahaṁ bhajāmi.*"

Kṛṣṇa was playing like a dramatic actor. Because Brahmā had some false prestige, thinking that he had some power, Kṛṣṇa showed him his real position. A similar incident occurred when Brahmā went to see Kṛṣṇa in Dvārakā. When Kṛṣṇa's doorman informed Lord Kṛṣṇa that Lord Brahmā had arrived, Kṛṣṇa responded, "Which Brahmā? Ask him which Brahmā." The doorman relayed this question, and Brahmā was astonished. "Is there another Brahmā besides me?" he thought. When the doorman informed Lord Kṛṣṇa, "It is four-headed Brahmā," Lord Kṛṣṇa said, "Oh, four-headed. Call others. Show him." This is Kṛṣṇa's position. For Kṛṣṇa the four-headed Brahmā is insignificant, to say nothing of "four-headed scientists." Materialistic scientists think that although this planet earth is full of opulence, all others are vacant. Because they simply speculate, this is their scientific conclusion. But from the *Bhāgavatam* we understand that the entire universe is full of living entities everywhere. Thus it is the folly of the scientists that although they do not know anything, they mislead people by presenting themselves as scientists, philosophers and men of knowledge.

TEXT 62

दृष्ट्वा त्वरेण निजधोरणतोऽवतीर्य
पृथ्व्यां वपुः कनकदण्डमिवाभिपात्य ।
स्पृष्ट्वा चतुर्मुकुटकोटिभिरङ्घ्रियुग्मं
नत्वा मुदश्रुसुजलैरकृताभिषेकम् ॥६२॥

dṛṣṭvā tvareṇa nija-dhoraṇato 'vatīrya
pṛthvyāṁ vapuḥ kanaka-daṇḍam ivābhipātya
spṛṣṭvā catur-mukuṭa-koṭibhir aṅghri-yugmaṁ
natvā mud-aśru-sujalair akṛtābhiṣekam

dṛṣṭvā—after seeing; *tvareṇa*—with great speed, hastily; *nija-dhoraṇataḥ*—from his swan carrier; *avatīrya*—descended; *pṛthvyām*—on the ground; *vapuḥ*—his body; *kanaka-daṇḍam iva*—like a golden rod; *abhipātya*—fell down; *spṛṣṭvā*—touching; *catuḥ-mukuṭa-koṭi-bhiḥ*—with the tips of his four crowns; *aṅghri-yugmam*—the two lotus feet; *natvā*—making obeisances; *mut-aśru-su-jalaiḥ*—with the water of his tears of joy; *akṛta*—performed; *abhiṣekam*—the ceremony of bathing His lotus feet.

TRANSLATION

After seeing this, Lord Brahmā hastily got down from his swan carrier, fell down like a golden rod and touched the lotus feet of Lord Kṛṣṇa with the tips of the four crowns on his heads. Offering his obeisances, he bathed the feet of Kṛṣṇa with the water of his tears of joy.

PURPORT

Lord Brahmā bowed down like a stick, and because Lord Brahmā's complexion is golden, he appeared to be like a golden stick lying down before Lord Kṛṣṇa. When one falls down before a superior just like a stick, one's offering of obeisances is called *daṇḍavat. Daṇḍa* means "stick," and *vat* means "like." It is not that one should simply say, "*daṇḍavat.*" Rather, one must fall down. Thus Brahmā fell down, touching his foreheads to the lotus feet of Kṛṣṇa, and his crying in ecstasy is to be regarded as an *abhiṣeka* bathing ceremony of Kṛṣṇa's lotus feet.

He who appeared before Brahmā as a human child was in fact the Absolute Truth, Parabrahman (*brahmeti paramātmeti bhagavān iti śabdyate*). The Supreme Lord is *narākṛti;* that is, He resembles a human being. It is not that He is four-armed (*catur-bāhu*). Nārāyaṇa is *catur-bāhu,* but the Supreme Person resembles a human being. This is also confirmed in the Bible, where it is said that man was made in the image of God.

Lord Brahmā saw that Kṛṣṇa, in His form as a cowherd boy, was Parabrahman, the root cause of everything, but was now appearing as a human child, loitering in Vṛndāvana with a morsel of food in His hand. Astonished, Lord Brahmā hastily got down from his swan carrier and let his body fall to the earth. Usually, the demigods never touch the ground, but Lord Brahmā, voluntarily giving up his prestige as a demigod, bowed down on the ground before Kṛṣṇa. Although Brahmā has one head in each direction, he voluntarily brought all his heads to the ground and touched Kṛṣṇa's feet with the tips of his four helmets. Although his intelligence works in every direction, he surrendered everything before the boy Kṛṣṇa.

It is mentioned that Brahmā washed the feet of Kṛṣṇa with his tears, and here the word *sujalaiḥ* indicates that his tears were purified. As soon as *bhakti* is present, everything is purified (*sarvopādhi-vinirmuktam*). Therefore Brahmā's crying was a form of *bhakty-anubhāva,* a transformation of transcendental ecstatic love.

TEXT 63

उत्थायोत्थाय कृष्णस्य चिरस्य पादयोः पतन् ।
आस्ते महित्वं प्राग्दृष्टं स्मृत्वा स्मृत्वा पुनः पुनः॥६३॥

utthāyotthāya kṛṣṇasya
cirasya pādayoḥ patan
āste mahitvaṁ prāg-dṛṣṭam
smṛtvā smṛtvā punaḥ punaḥ

utthāya utthāya—rising repeatedly; *kṛṣṇasya*—of Lord Kṛṣṇa; *cirasya*—for a long time; *pādayoḥ*—at the lotus feet; *patan*—falling down; *āste*—remained; *mahitvam*—the greatness; *prāk-dṛṣṭam*—which he had previously seen; *smṛtvā smṛtvā*—remembering and remembering; *punaḥ punaḥ*—again and again.

TRANSLATION

Rising and falling again and again at the lotus feet of Lord Kṛṣṇa for a long time, Lord Brahmā remembered over and over the Lord's greatness he had just seen.

PURPORT

As stated in one prayer,

śrutim apare smṛtim itare
bhāratam anye bhajantu bhava-bhītāḥ
aham iha nandaṁ vande
yasyālinde paraṁ brahma

"Let others study the *Vedas*, *smṛti* and *Mahābhārata*, fearing material existence, but I shall worship Nanda Mahārāja, in whose courtyard is crawling the Supreme Brahman. Nanda Mahārāja is so great that the Parabrahman is crawling in his yard, and therefore I shall worship him." (*Padyāvali* 126)

Brahmā was falling down in ecstasy. Because of the presence of the Supreme Personality of Godhead, who exactly resembled a human child, Brahmā was naturally astonished. Therefore with a faltering voice he offered prayers, understanding that here was the Supreme Person.

TEXT 64

शनैरथोत्थाय विमृज्य लोचने
मुकुन्दमुद्वीक्ष्य विनम्रकन्धरः ।
कृताञ्जलिः प्रश्रयवान् समाहितः
सवेपथुर्गद्गदयैलतेलया ॥६४॥

śanair athotthāya vimṛjya locane
mukundam udvīkṣya vinamra-kandharaḥ
kṛtāñjaliḥ praśrayavān samāhitaḥ
sa-vepathur gadgadayailatelayā

śanaiḥ—gradually; *atha*—then; *utthāya*—rising; *vimṛjya*—wiping; *locane*—his two eyes; *mukundam*—at Mukunda, Lord Śrī Kṛṣṇa; *udvīkṣya*—looking up; *vinamra-kandharaḥ*—his neck bent; *kṛta-añjaliḥ*—with folded hands; *praśraya-vān*—very humble; *samāhitaḥ*—his mind concentrated; *sa-vepathuḥ*—his body trembling; *gadgadayā*—faltering; *ailata*—Brahmā began to offer praise; *īlayā*—with words.

TRANSLATION

Then, rising very gradually and wiping his two eyes, Lord Brahmā looked up at Mukunda. Lord Brahmā, his head bent low, his mind concentrated and his body trembling, very humbly began, with faltering words, to offer praises to Lord Kṛṣṇa.

PURPORT

Brahmā, being very joyful, began to shed tears, and he washed the lotus feet of Kṛṣṇa with his tears. Repeatedly he fell and rose as he recalled the wonderful activities of the Lord. After repeating obeisances for a long time, Brahmā stood up and smeared his hands over his eyes. Śrīla Viśvanātha Cakravartī Ṭhākura comments that the word *locane* indicates that with his two hands he wiped the two eyes on each of his four faces. Seeing the Lord before him, Brahmā began to offer prayers with great humility, respect and attention.

Thus end the Bhaktivedanta purports of the Tenth Canto, Thirteenth Chapter, of the Śrīmad-Bhāgavatam, *entitled "The Stealing of the Boys and Calves by Brahmā."*

Appendixes

The Author

His Divine Grace A. C. Bhaktivedanta Swami Prabhupāda appeared in this world in 1896 in Calcutta, India. He first met his spiritual master, Śrīla Bhaktisiddhānta Sarasvatī Gosvāmī, in Calcutta in 1922. Bhaktisiddhānta Sarasvatī, a prominent religious scholar and the founder of sixty-four Gauḍīya Maṭhas (Vedic institutes), liked this educated young man and convinced him to dedicate his life to teaching Vedic knowledge. Śrīla Prabhupāda became his student, and eleven years later (1933) at Allahabad he became his formally initiated disciple.

At their first meeting, in 1922, Śrīla Bhaktisiddhānta Sarasvatī Ṭhākura requested Śrīla Prabhupāda to broadcast Vedic knowledge through the English language. In the years that followed, Śrīla Prabhupāda wrote a commentary on the *Bhagavad-gītā*, assisted the Gauḍīya Maṭha in its work and, in 1944, without assistance, started an English fortnightly magazine, edited it, typed the manuscripts and checked the galley proofs. He even distributed the individual copies and struggled to maintain the publication. Once begun, the magazine never stopped; it is now being continued by his disciples in the West and is published in nineteen languages.

Recognizing Śrīla Prabhupāda's philosophical learning and devotion, the Gauḍīya Vaiṣṇava Society honored him in 1947 with the title "Bhaktivedanta." In 1950, at the age of fifty-four, Śrīla Prabhupāda retired from married life, adopting the *vānaprastha* (retired) order to devote more time to his studies and writing. Śrīla Prabhupāda traveled to the holy city of Vṛndāvana, where he lived in very humble circumstances in the historic medieval temple of Rādhā-Dāmodara. There he engaged for several years in deep study and writing. He accepted the renounced order of life (*sannyāsa*) in 1959. At Rādhā-Dāmodara, Śrīla Prabhupāda began work on his life's masterpiece: a multivolume translation of and commentary on the eighteen-thousand-verse *Śrīmad-Bhāgavatam* (*Bhāgavata Purāṇa*). He also wrote *Easy Journey to Other Planets.*

After publishing three volumes of the *Bhāgavatam*, Śrīla Prabhupāda came to the United States, in 1965, to fulfill the mission of his spiritual master. Subsequently, His Divine Grace wrote more than sixty volumes of authoritative translations, commentaries and summary studies of the philosophical and religious classics of India.

In 1965, when he first arrived by freighter in New York City, Śrīla Prabhupāda was practically penniless. It was after almost a year of great difficulty that he established the International Society for Krishna Consciousness in July of 1966. Before his passing away on November 14, 1977, he guided the Society and saw it grow to a worldwide confederation of more than one hundred *āśramas*, schools, temples, institutes and farm communities.

In 1968, Śrīla Prabhupāda created New Vrindaban, an experimental Vedic community in the hills of West Virginia. Inspired by the success of New Vrindaban, now a thriving farm community of more than one thousand acres, his students have since founded several similar communities in the United States and abroad.

In 1972, His Divine Grace introduced the Vedic system of primary and secondary education in the West by founding the Gurukula school in Dallas, Texas. Since then, under his supervision, his disciples have established children's schools throughout the United States and the rest of the world. As of 1978, there are ten *gurukula* schools worldwide, with the principal educational center now located in Vṛndāvana, India.

Śrīla Prabhupāda also inspired the construction of several large international cultural centers in India. The center at Śrīdhāma Māyāpur in West Bengal is the site for a planned spiritual city, an ambitious project for which construction will extend over the next decade. In Vṛndāvana, India, is the magnificent Kṛṣṇa-Balarāma Temple and International Guesthouse. There is also a major cultural and educational center in Bombay. Other centers are planned in a dozen other important locations on the Indian subcontinent.

Śrīla Prabhupāda's most significant contribution, however, is his books. Highly respected by the academic community for their authoritativeness, depth and clarity, they are used as standard textbooks in numerous college courses. His writings have been translated into twenty-eight languages. The Bhaktivedanta Book Trust, established in 1972 exclusively to publish the works of His Divine Grace, has thus become the world's largest publisher of books in the field of Indian religion and philosophy.

In just twelve years, in spite of his advanced age, Śrīla Prabhupāda circled the globe fourteen times on lecture tours that took him to six continents. In spite of such a vigorous schedule, Śrīla Prabhupāda continued to write prolifically. His writings constitute a veritable library of Vedic philosophy, religion, literature and culture.

References

The purports of *Śrīmad-Bhāgavatam* are all confirmed by standard Vedic authorities. The following authentic scriptures are specifically cited in this volume:

Bhagavad-gītā, 17, 40, 55, 58, 59, 68

Brahma-saṁhitā, 3, 21, 40, 47

Bṛhad-āraṇyaka Upaniṣad, 68

Caitanya-caritāmṛta, 54–55, 56, 57, 67, 70

Muṇḍaka Upaniṣad, 60

Padyāvali, 77

Śrīmad-Bhāgavatam, 13, 14, 17, 52, 57, 58, 61, 62, 71

Śvetāśvatara Upaniṣad, 15, 61, 66

Glossary

A

Abhiṣeka—a bathing ceremony, particularly for the coronation of a king or the installation of the Lord's Deity form.

Ācārya—a spiritual master who teaches by example.

Acintya-bhedābheda-tattva—the philosophy of the inconceivably simultaneous oneness and difference of the Lord and His creation, first propagated by Śrī Caitanya Mahāprabhu.

Advaita-vādīs—*See:* Māyāvādīs

Aghāsura—the python-shaped demon sent by Kaṁsa to kill Kṛṣṇa.

B

Balarāma (Baladeva)—a plenary expansion of the Personality of Godhead, appearing as the son of Rohiṇī and elder brother of Lord Kṛṣṇa.

Bhagavad-gītā—the battlefield discourse between the Supreme Lord, Kṛṣṇa, and His devotee Arjuna expounding devotional service as both the principal means and the ultimate end of spiritual perfection.

Bhakta—a devotee of the Supreme Lord, Kṛṣṇa.

Bhakti-yoga—linking with the Supreme Lord by devotional service.

Brahmā—the first created living being and secondary creator of the material universe.

Brāhmaṇa—one wise in the *Vedas* who can guide society; the first Vedic social order.

C

Caitanya Mahāprabhu—the incarnation of Lord Kṛṣṇa who descended to teach love of God through the *saṅkīrtana* movement.

Catur-bhuja—four-armed.

G

Gokula—*See:* Vṛndāvana

Gopīs—Kṛṣṇa's cowherd girl friends, His most confidential servitors.

Gosvāmī—one who has become master of his own senses.

J

Jīva-tattva—the individual living entities, who are atomic parts of the Lord.

Jñānī—one who cultivates transcendental knowledge by empirical speculation.

M

Mahābhārata—Vyāsadeva's epic history of the Kurukṣetra war.

Mahāmāyā—*See: Māyā*

Mahat-tattva—the total material energy in its original, undifferentiated form.

Maṅgala-ārātrika—the daily early-morning ceremony of worship for the Deity of the Supreme Lord.

Mantra—a Vedic sound vibration that can deliver the mind from illusion.

Māyā—the inferior, illusory energy of the Supreme Lord, which rules over this material creation; also, forgetfulness of one's relationship with Kṛṣṇa.

Māyāvādīs—impersonal philosophers who say that the Supreme Lord cannot have a spiritual body.

Mlecchas—uncivilized humans, outside the Vedic system of society, who are generally meat-eaters.

Mukunda—a name of the Supreme Personality of Godhead, who is the giver of liberation.

N

Nārāyaṇa—a name of the Supreme Personality of Godhead, who is the source and goal of all living beings.

P

Parabrahman—the Supreme Absolute Truth as the Personality of Godhead, Viṣṇu, or Kṛṣṇa.

Paramahaṁsa—"topmost swan"; a person on the highest platform of God consciousness.

Paramātmā—Lord Viṣṇu as the Supersoul present within the heart of every individual living being.

Paramparā—a disciplic succession of spiritual masters.

Prakṛti—material nature.

Prasāda—"the Lord's mercy"; food which has become spiritualized by first being offered for God's pleasure.

R

Rajo-guṇa—passion, one of the three modes which control material existence.

Rāvaṇa—the demoniac ruler who was killed by Lord Rāmacandra.

S

Sādhana—the beginning phase of devotional service as regulated practice.

Sādhus—saintly persons.

Śaṅkarācārya—the incarnation of Lord Śiva who, ordered by the Supreme Lord, propagated the famous Māyāvāda philosophy, which maintains that there is no distinction between the Lord and the living entities.

Sārūpya-mukti—the liberation of achieving a spiritual form similar to that of the Supreme Lord.

Śāstras—revealed scriptures, such as the Vedic literature.

Sītā—the eternal consort of Lord Rāmacandra.

Śiva—the demigod in charge of the mode of ignorance and the destruction of the material manifestation.

Smṛti—supplementary Vedic scriptures, apart from the original *Vedas.*

Śuddha-sattva—the transcendental platform of "pure goodness," beyond the material modes of goodness, passion and ignorance.

T

Tamo-guṇa—ignorance, one of the three modes which control material existence.

Tilaka—auspicious clay marks that sanctify a devotee's body as a temple of the Lord.

Tulasī—the sacred plant whose leaves are especially dear to Lord Kṛṣṇa.

U

Upaniṣads—the philosophic portions of the *Vedas.*

V

Vaikuṇṭha—the kingdom of God, which is "free from anxiety."

Vaiṣṇava—a devotee of the Supreme Lord, Viṣṇu, or Kṛṣṇa.

Vedānta—the summary presentation of "the final conclusion of Vedic knowledge," compiled by Śrī Vyāsadeva in concise codes.

Vedas—the original revealed scriptures, first spoken by the Lord Himself.

Viṣṇu—Lord Kṛṣṇa's expansions in Vaikuṇṭha and for the creation and maintenance of the material universes.

Viṣṇu-mūrtis—forms of the Supreme Lord.

Viṣṇu-tattva—the different direct expansions of the Lord, each of whom is the same Supreme Person.

Vraja(bhūmi)—*See:* Vṛndāvana

Vṛndāvana—Kṛṣṇa's eternal abode, where He fully manifests His quality of sweetness; the village on this earth in which He appeared five thousand years ago.

Y

Yajña—sacrifice performed for the satisfaction of the Supreme Lord.

Yavanas—barbarians.

Yogī—a transcendentalist who, in one way or another, is striving for union with the Supreme.

Sanskrit Pronunciation Guide

Vowels

अ a आ ā इ i ई ī उ u ऊ ū ऋ ṛ ॠ ṝ
ऌ ḷ ए e ऐ ai ओ o औ au

ं ṁ (*anusvāra*) ः ḥ (*visarga*)

Consonants

Gutturals:	क ka	ख kha	ग ga	घ gha	ङ ṅa
Palatals:	च ca	छ cha	ज ja	झ jha	ञ ña
Cerebrals:	ट ṭa	ठ ṭha	ड ḍa	ढ ḍha	ण ṇa
Dentals:	त ta	थ tha	द da	ध dha	न na
Labials:	प pa	फ pha	ब ba	भ bha	म ma
Semivowels:	य ya	र ra	ल la	व va	
Sibilants:	श śa	ष ṣa	स sa		
Aspirate:	ह ha	ऽ ' (*avagraha*) – the apostrophe			

The numerals are: ० -0 १ -1 २ -2 ३ -3 ४ -4 ५ -5 ६ -6 ७ -7 ८ -8 ९ -9

The vowels above should be pronounced as follows:

a – like the *a* in org*a*n or the *u* in b*u*t
ā – like the *a* in f*a*r but held twice as long as short *a*
i – like the *i* in p*i*n
ī – like the *i* in p*i*que but held twice as long as short *i*

u – like the *u* in push.
ū – like the *u* in r*u*le but held twice as long as short *u*.
ṛ – like the *ri* in *ri*m.
ṝ – like *ree* in *ree*d.
ḷ – like *l* followed by *ṛ* (*lṛ*).
e – like the *e* in th*e*y.
ai – like the *ai* in *ai*sle.
o – like the *o* in g*o*.
au – like the *ow* in h*ow*.
ṁ (*anusvāra*) – a resonant nasal like the *n* in the French word *bon*.
ḥ (*visarga*) – a final *h*-sound: *aḥ* is pronounced like *aha; iḥ* like *ihi*.

The vowels are written as follows after a consonant:

ा ā ि i ी ī ु u ू ū ृ ṛ ॄ ṝ े e ै ai ो o ौ au

For example: क ka का kā कि ki की kī कु ku कू kū
कृ kṛ कॄ kṝ के ke कै kai को ko कौ kau

The vowel "a" is implied after a consonant with no vowel symbol.

The symbol virāma (्) indicates that there is no final vowel: क्

The consonants are pronounced as follows:

k – as in *k*ite
kh – as in Ec*kh*art
g – as in *g*ive
gh – as in di*g-h*ard
ṅ – as in si*ng*
c – as in *ch*air
ch – as in staun*ch-h*eart
j – as in *j*oy
jh – as in he*dgeh*og
ñ – as in ca*ny*on
ṭ – as in *t*ub
ṭh – as in ligh*t-h*eart
ḍ – as in *d*ove
ḍha- as in re*d-h*ot
ṇ – as r*na* (prepare to say the *r* and say *na*).

t – as in *t*ub but with tongue against teeth.
th – as in ligh*t-h*eart but with tongue against teeth.

d – as in *d*ove but with tongue against teeth
dh – as in re*d-h*ot but with tongue against teeth
n – as in *n*ut but with tongue between teeth
p – as in *p*ine
ph – as in u*ph*ill (not *f*)
b – as in *b*ird
bh – as in ru*b-h*ard
m – as in *m*other
y – as in *y*es
r – as in *r*un
l – as in *l*ight
v – as in *v*ine
ś (palatal) – as in the *s* in the German word *sprechen*
ṣ (cerebral) – as the *sh* in *sh*ine
s – as in *s*un
h – as in *h*ome

Generally two or more consonants in conjunction are written together in a special form, as for example: क्ष kṣa त्र tra

There is no strong accentuation of syllables in Sanskrit, or pausing between words in a line, only a flowing of short and long (twice as long as the short) syllables. A long syllable is one whose vowel is long (ā, ī, ū, e, ai, o, au), or whose short vowel is followed by more than one consonant (including anusvāra and visarga). Aspirated consonants (such as kha and gha) count as only single consonants.

ISKCON Centers Around the World

AFRICA
Durban (Natal), S. Africa—P.O. Box 212, Cato Ridge, Natal 3680 / Cato Ridge 237; **Johannesburg, S. Africa**—Elberta Rd., Honeydew (mail: P.O. Box 5302, Weltevreden Park 1715) / 6752845; **Lagos, Nigeria**—P.O. Box 8793, West Africa; **Mauritius**—10 E. Serret St., Rose Hill (mail: P.O. Box 718, Port Louis, Mauritius); **Mombasa, Kenya, E. Africa**—Madhavani House, Sauti Ya Kenya and Kisumu Rd., P.O. Box 82224 / 312248; **Nairobi, Kenya, E. Africa**—Muhoroni Close, P.O. Box 28946 / 331568.

ASIA
INDIA: **Ahmedabad, Gujarat**—7, Kailas Society, Ashram Rd., 380 009 / 49935; **Bangalore, Mysore**—40 Hare Krishna Rd., 560 001 / 77664; **Bhadrak, Orissa**—Gour Gopal Mandir, Kuans, P.O. Bhadrak, Dist. Balasore; **Bhubaneswar, Orissa**—National Highway No. 5, Nayapalli (mail: c/o P.O. Box 173, 751 001) / 53125; **Bombay, Maharastra**—Hare Krishna Land, Juhu, 400 054 / 566-860; **Calcutta, W. Bengal**—3 Albert Rd., 700 017 / 44-3757; **Chandigarh, Punjab**—Hare Krishna Land, Dakshin Marg, Sector 36-B, 160 023; **Chhaygharia (Haridaspur), W. Bengal**—Thakur Haridas Sripatbari Sevashram, P.O. Chhaygharia, P.S. Bongaon, Dist. 24 Pargonas; **Gauhati, Assam**—Post Bag No. 127, 781 001; **Hyderabad, A.P.**—Hare Krishna Land, Nampally Station Rd., 500 001 / 51018; **Imphal, Manipur**—Paona Bazar, 795 001; **Madras, Tamil Nadu**—4 Srinivasamurty Ave., Adayar, Madras 20; **Mayapur, W. Bengal**—Shree Mayapur Chandrodaya Mandir, P.O. Shree Mayapur Dham (District Nadia); **New Delhi, U.P.**—M-119 Greater Kailash 1, 110 048 / 624-590; **Patna, Bihar**—Post Bag 173, Patna 800 001; **Vrindavan, U.P.**—Krishna-Balarama Mandir, Bhaktivedanta Swami Marg, Raman Reti, Mathura / 178.
FARMS: **Hyderabad, A.P.**—P.O. Dabilpur Village, Medchal Taluq, Hyderabad District, 501 401; **Mayapur, W. Bengal**—(contact ISKCON Mayapur).
RESTAURANTS: **Bombay**—Hare Krishna Land; **Mayapur**—Shree Mayapur Chandrodaya Mandir; **Vrindavan**—Krishna-Balarama Mandir.
OTHER COUNTRIES: **Bangkok, Thailand**—P.O. Box 12-1108; **Butterworth, Malaysia**—1 Lintang Melur, M.K. 14, Butterworth, Province Wellesley / 04-331019; **Colombo, Sri Lanka**—188, New Chetty St., Colombo 13 / 33325; **Hong Kong**—5 Homantin St., Flat 23, Kowloon / 3-029113; **Kathmandu, Nepal**—8/6, Battis Putali, Goshalla; **Mandaue City, Philippines**—231 Pagsabungan Rd., Basak, Cebu / 83254; **Selangor, Malaysia**—No. 18 Jalan 6/6, Petaling Jaya / 564957; **Tehran, Iran**—Felistin Ave. (old Kakh), Shemshad St., No. 3 / 644-272; **Tel Aviv, Israel**—147 Hanassi St., Herzliya Pituah / 938-846.

AUSTRALASIA
Adelaide, Australia—13-A Frome St. / (08)223-2084; **Auckland, New Zealand**—Hwy. 18, Riverhead (next to Huapai Golfcourse) (mail: c/o R.D. 2, Kumeu) / 412-8075; **Jakarta, Indonesia**—Jalan Rawamangun Muka Timur 80 / 4835-19; **Lautoka, Fiji**—5 Tavewa Ave. (mail: c/o P.O. Box 125) / 61-633, ext. 48; **Melbourne, Australia**—197 Danks St., Albert Park, Melbourne, Victoria 3206 (mail: c/o P.O. Box 125) / 699-5122; **Perth, Australia**—P.O. Box 299, Subiaco, 6008, Perth, Western Australia; **Sydney, Australia**—112 Darlinghurst Rd., King's Cross, N.S.W. (mail: c/o P.O. Box 159) / (02)357-5162.
FARMS: **Auckland, New Zealand (New Varshana)**—contact ISKCON Auckland; **Colo, Australia (Bhaktivedanta Ashram)**—Upper Colo Rd., N.S.W. (mail: c/o P.O. Box 493, St. Mary's, 2760, N.S.W.) / 045-75-5284; **Murwillumbah, Australia (New Govardhana)**—'Eungella,' Tyalgum Rd. via Murwillumbah, N.S.W. 2484 (mail: c/o P.O. Box 687) / 066-72-1903.
RESTAURANTS: **Adelaide**—Govinda's, 13 Frome Street; **Melbourne**—Gopal's, 237 Flinders Lane / 63 1578; **Melbourne**—Gopal's, 251 Malvern Road, South Yarrow; **Sydney**—Mukunda's, 233 Victoria Street, Darlinghurst / 357 5162.

EUROPE
Amsterdam, Holland—Keizersgracht 94 / 020-249 410; **Antwerp, Belgium**—25 Katelijnevest / 031-320987; **Athens, Greece**—133 Solonos; **Catania, Sicily**—Via Empedocle 84, 95100 / 095-522-252; **Copenhagen, Denmark**—Korfuvej 9, 2300 Copenhagen S / 972337; **Dublin, Ireland**—2 Belvedere Place, Dublin 1 / 743-767; **Duedingen, Switzerland**—Im Stillen Tal, CH 3186 Duedingen (FR) / (037) 43.26.97; **Gallarate, Italy**—Via A. Volta 19, Gallarate 20131 (VA) / 0331-783-268; **Göthenburg, Sweden**—Karl Gustavsgatan 19, 41125 Göthenburg / 031-110955; **Heidelberg, W. Germany**—Vrindavana, Plöck 54; **London, England (city)**—10 Soho St., London W1 / 01-437-1835; **London, England (country)**—Bhaktivedanta Manor, Letchmore Heath, Watford, Hertfordshire WD2 8EP / Radlett 7244; **Madrid, Spain**—Calle Arturo Sorio No. 209; **Munich, W. Germany**—Govinda's Club, Kaulbachstrasse 1, 8000 München / 089-280807; **Paris, France**—20 rue Vieille du Temple, Paris 75004 / 500-63-58; **Rome, Italy**—Salita del Poggio Laurentino 7, Rome 00144 / (06)593-075; **Septon, Belgium**—Chateau de Petit Somme, Septon 5482 / 086-322480; **Stockholm, Sweden**—Korsnas Gård, 140 32 Grodinge / 0753-29151; **Vienna, Austria**—Govinda Kulturzentrum, Lerchenfelderstrasse 17, A-1070 Wien / (0222) 96 10 633; **West Berlin, W. Germany**—Karl Marx Strasse 17, Neu Kölln / 030-6231984; **Worcester, England**—Chaitanya College at Croome Court, Severn Stoke, Worcester WR8 9DW / 090 567-214; **Zurich, Switzerland**—Bergstrasse 54, 8032 Zürich / (01)693388.
FARMS: **Bavarian Forest (Bayrische-Wald), W. Germany (Nava-Jiyada-Nṛsiṁha-Kṣetra)**—(contact ISKCON Munich); **Brihuega, Spain (New Vraja Maṇḍala)**—(Santa Clara) Brihuega, Guadalajara / (11) 280018; **Firenze, Italy (Villa Vṛndāvana)**—Via Comunale degli Scopeti, No. 106, St. Andrea in Percussina, San Casciano Val di Pesa 56030 (Firenze) / 055-820054; **London, England**—(contact Bhaktivedanta Manor); **Valencay, France (New Māyāpur)**—Lucay-Le-Male, 36 600 / (54) 40-23-26.
RESTAURANTS: **London**—Healthy, Wealthy, and Wise, 9-10 Soho Street; **Stockholm**—Govinda's, Grevgatan 18, 114 53 Stockholm / 08-623411; **Vienna**—Govinda (at ISKCON Vienna); **Zurich**—Govinda, Brandschenkestrasse 12, 8002 Zurich / (01)2029282.

LATIN AMERICA
BRAZIL: **Curitiba, Paraná**—Rua Profa. Maria Assumpaco 77, Vila Hauer, 80.000 / 276-6274; **Pôrto Alegre, RS**—Rua Giordano Bruno 318, 90.000; **Recife, Pernambuco**—Ave. 17 de Agosto 257, Parnamirim 50.000; **Rio de Janeiro, RJ**—Estrada dos Tres Rios 654, Jacarepagua, 22.700; **Salvador, Bahia**—Rua Alvaro Adorno 17, Brotas, 40.000 / (071)240-1072; **São Paulo, SP**—Rua Pandia Calogeras 54, 01525 / (011)270-3442.
FARM: **Pindamonhangaba, São Paulo (New Gokula)**—Ribeirao Grande (mail: C.P. 108, 12.400 Pindamonhangaba) / 2797836.
OTHER COUNTRIES: **Bogotá, Colombia**—Carrera 3A No. 54-A-72 / 255-9842; **Cuzco, Peru**—Avenida Pardo No. 1036 / 2277; **Georgetown, Guyana**—24 Uitvlugt Front, West Coast Demerara; **Guadalajara, Mexico**—Avenida las Americas No. 225, Sector Hidalgo / 163455; **Guatemala City, Guatemala**—Sexta Avenida 1-89, Zona 1 / 24618; **La Paz, Bolivia**—Calle Chacaltaya No. 587 / 32-85-67; **Lima, Peru**—Jiron Junin 415 / 47-18-10; **Medellin, Colombia**—Carrera 32, No. 54-42; **Mexico City, Mexico**—Gob. Tiburcio Montiel 45, San Miguel Chapultepec, Mexico D.F. 18 / (905)271-0132; **Monterrey, Mexico**—General Albino Espinoza, 345 Pte., Zona Centro, Monterrey, N.L. / 42 67 66; **Panama City, Panama**—43-58 Via España Altos, Al Lado del Cine, Bella Vista; **Puebla, Mexico**—Sierra Madre 9010, Colonia Maravillas, Puebla; **Quito, Ecuador**—Apdo. 2384, Calle Yasuni No. 404; **St. Augustine, Trinidad and Tobago**—Gordon St. at Santa Margarita Circular Rd. / 662-4605; **San José, Costa Rica**—400 mtrs. Sur Centro Médico de Guadalupe (casa blanca esquinera) Colonia Chapultepec, Guadalupe; **San Salvador, El Salvador**—67 Avenida Sur No. 115, Colonia Escalo; **Santiago, Chile**—Eyzaguirre 2404, Casilla 44, Puente Alto / 283; **Santo Domingo, Dominican Republic**—Calle Cayatano Rodriguez No. 36 / (809)688-7242; **Valparaiso, Chile**—Colon 2706 / 7099; **Vera Cruz, Mexico**—Calle 3 Carabelas No. 784, Fraccionmiento Reforma, Vera Cruz.

NORTH AMERICA
CANADA: **Edmonton, Alberta**—10132 142nd St., T5N 2N7 / (403)452-5855; **Montreal, Quebec**—1626 Pie IX Boulevard, H1V 2C5 / (514) 527-1101; **Ottawa, Ontario**—212 Somerset St. E., K1N 6V4 / (613)233-3460; **Toronto, Ontario**—243 Avenue Rd. M5R 2J6 / (416)922-5415; **Vancouver, B.C.**—5580 S.E. Marine Dr., Burnaby V5J 3G8 / (604)430-4437; **Victoria, B.C.**—4056 Rainbow St., V8X 2A9 / (604)479-0649.
FARM: **Hemingford, Quebec (New Nandagram)**—315 Backbrush Rd., RR. No. 2, J0L 1H0 / (514)247-3429.
RESTAURANTS: **Toronto**—Govinda's, 1280 Bay St. / (416)968-1313; **Vancouver**—Govinda's, 1221 Thurlow / (604)682-8154.
U.S.A.: **Atlanta, Georgia**—1287 Ponce de Leon Ave. NE 30306 / (404)378-9182; **Austin, Texas**—1910 Whitis Ave. 78705 / (512)476-7138; **Baltimore, Maryland**—200 Bloomsbury Ave., Catonsville 21228 / (301)788-3883; **Berkeley, California**—2334 Stuart St. 94705 / (415) 843-7874; **Boston, Massachusetts**—72 Commonwealth Ave. 02116 / (617)536-1695; **Chicago, Illinois**—1716 West Lunt Ave. 60626 / (312)973-0900; **Cleveland, Ohio**—15720 Euclid Ave., E. Cleveland 44112 / (216)851-9367; **Columbus, Ohio**—99 East 13th Ave. 43201 / (614) 299-5084; **Dallas, Texas**—5430 Gurley Ave. 75223 / (214)827-6330; **Denver, Colorado**—1400 Cherry St. 80220 / (303)333-5461; **Detroit, Michigan**—383 Lenox Ave. 48215 / (313)824-6000; **E. Lansing, Michigan**—319 Grove St. 48823 / (517)351-6603; **Gainesville, Florida**—921 S.W. Depot Ave. 32601 / (904)-377-1496; **Hartford, Connecticut**—1683 Main St., East Hartford 06108 / (203)-528-1600; **Honolulu, Hawaii**—51 Coelho Way 96817 / (808)595-3947; **Houston, Texas**—1111 Rosalie St. 77004 / (713)526-9860; **Laguna Beach, California**—644 S. Coast Hwy. 92651 / (714)497-3638; **Las Vegas, Nevada**—5605 Alta Dr. 87066 (702)870-6638; **Long Island, New York**—197 S. Ocean Ave., Freeport 11520 / (516)378-6184; **Los Angeles, California**—3764 Watseka Ave. 90034 / (213) 871-0717; **Miami Beach, Florida**—2445 Collins Ave. 33140 / (305)531-0331; **Newark, Delaware**—168 Elkton Rd. 19711 / (302)453-8510; **New Orleans, Louisiana**—2936 Esplanade Ave. 70119 / (504)488-7433; **New York, New York**—340 W. 55th St. 10019 / (212)765-8610; **Philadelphia, Pennsylvania**—41-51 West Allens Lane, 19119 / (215)247-4600; **Pittsburgh, Pennsylvania**—1112 N. Negley Ave. 15026 / (412)362-0212; **Portland, Oregon**—2805 S.E. Hawthorne St. 97214 / (503)231-5792; **St. Louis, Missouri**—3926 Lindell Blvd. 63108 / (314)535-8085; **San Diego, California**—1030 Grand Ave., Pacific Beach 92109 / (714)483-2500; **San Juan, Puerto Rico**—1016 Ponce de Leon St., Rio Piedras, 00925 / (809)-765-4745; **Seattle, Washington**—400 18th Ave. East 98112 / (206)322-3636; **State College, Pennsylvania**—103 E. Hamilton Ave. 16801 / (814)234-1867; **Washington, D.C.**—10310 Oaklyn Rd., Potomac, Maryland 20854 / (301)-299-2100.

FARMS: **Carriere, Mississippi (New Tālavan)**—Rt. No. 2, Box 449, 39426 / (601)798-6705; **Gainesville, Florida**—contact ISKCON Gainesville; **Gurabo, Puerto Rico (New Gandhamadana)**—Box 215 B, Route 181, Santarita 00658; **Hopland, California (New Vraja-maṇḍala Dhāma)**—Route 175, Box 469, 95449 / (707)744-1100; **Hotchkiss, Colorado (New Barshana)**—P.O. Box 112, 81419 / (303)527-4584; **Lynchburg, Tennessee (Murāri-sevaka)**—Rt. No. 1, Box 146-A, (Mulberry) 37359 / (615)759-7058; **Moundsville, West Virginia (New Vrindaban)**—R.D. No. 1, Box 319, Hare Krishna Ridge 26041 / (304)845-2790; **Port Royal, Pennsylvania (Gītā-nāgari)**—R.D. No. 1, 17082 / (717)527-2493.
RESTAURANTS: **Austin, Texas**—Govinda's (at ISKCON Austin); **Columbus, Ohio**—Simply Wonderful, 2044 High Street 43201 / (614)299-6132; **Los Angeles**—Govinda's, 9634 Venice Blvd., 90230 / (213)836-1269; **New York, New York**—Govinda's (at ISKCON New York); **St. Louis, Missouri**—(at ISKCON St. Louis) / (341)535-8161; **San Juan, Puerto Rico**—Govinda's (at ISKCON San Juan); **Washington, D.C.**—Govinda's, 515 8th St. S.E. 20003 / (202)543-9600.

Index of Sanskrit Verses

This index constitutes a complete listing of the first and third lines of each of the Sanskrit poetry verses of this volume of *Śrīmad-Bhāgavatam*, arranged in English alphabetical order. The first column gives the Sanskrit transliteration, and the second and third columns, respectively, list the chapter-verse reference and page number for each verse.

A

aho 'tiramyaṁ pulinaṁ vayasyāḥ	13.5	6
ambhojanma-janis tad-antara-gato	13.15	15
aṅghri-mastakam āpūrṇās	13.49	51
aṇimādyair mahimabhir	13.52	55
anīśe 'pi draṣṭuṁ kim idam iti vā	13.57	65
aspṛṣṭa-bhūri-māhātmyā	13.54	60
āste mahitvaṁ prāg-dṛṣṭam	13.63	76
ātmādi-stamba-paryantair	13.51	54
atra bhoktavyam asmābhir	13.6	7

B

bhārataivaṁ vatsa-peṣu	13.12	12
bibhrad veṇuṁ jaṭhara-paṭayoḥ	13.11	11
brūyuḥ snigdhasya śiṣyasya	13.3	5

C

candrikā-viśada-smeraiḥ	13.50	52
catur-bhujāḥ śaṅkha-cakra-	13.47	50
catur-viṁśatibhis tattvaiḥ	13.52	55

D

dṛṣṭvātha tat-sneha-vaśo 'smṛtātmā	13.30	30
dṛṣṭvā tvareṇa nija-dhoraṇato	13.62	75
durgādhva-kṛcchrato 'bhyetya	13.32	32
dvi-pāt kukud-grīva udāsya-puccho	13.30	30

E

ekadā cārayan vatsān	13.28	29
evam eteṣu bhedeṣu	13.43	44
evaṁ sakṛd dadarśājaḥ	13.55	63
evaṁ sammohayan viṣṇuṁ	13.44	45

G

gāvas tato goṣṭham upetya satvaraṁ	13.24	26
gilantya iva cāṅgāni	13.31	31
go-gopīnāṁ mātṛtāsminn	13.25	27
gopās tad-rodhanāyāsa-	13.32	32
govardhanādri-śirasi	13.29	30

H

hasanto hāsayantaś cā-	13.10	10

I

ita ete 'tra kutratyā	13.42	43
itīreśe 'tarkye nija-mahimani	13.57	65
iti sañcintya dāśārho	13.38	38
ittham ātmātmanātmānaṁ	13.27	28
ity uktvādri-darī-kuñja-	13.14	14

K

kāla-svabhāva-saṁskāra-	13.53	56
kecit puṣpair dalaiḥ kecit	13.9	9
keyaṁ vā kuta āyātā	13.37	37
kim etad adbhutam iva	13.36	36
kirīṭinaḥ kuṇḍalino	13.47	50
komalaiḥ sarva-gātreṣu	13.49	51
kṛcchrāc chanair apagatās	13.34	34
kṛcchrād unmīlya vai dṛṣṭīr	13.58	69
krīḍann ātma-vihāraiś ca	13.20	22
kṛṣṇasya viṣvak puru-rāji-maṇḍalair	13.8	8

kṛtāñjaliḥ praśrayavān samāhitaḥ	13.64	78
kvāpy adṛṣṭvāntar-vipine	13.17	18

M

mahatītara-māyaiśyaṁ	13.45	48
māyāśaye śayānā me	13.41	43
mitrāṇīvājitāvāsa-	13.60	71
mitrāṇy āśān viramate-	13.13	13
mukta-staneṣv apatyeṣv apy	13.35	35
muktvā śikyāni bubhujuḥ	13.7	8

N

naite sureśā ṛṣayo na caite	13.39	38
nītvānyatra kurūdvahāntaradadhāt	13.15	15
nṛtya-gītādy-anekārhaiḥ	13.51	54
nūpuraiḥ kaṭakair bhātāḥ	13.48	50

P

pālayan vatsapo varṣam	13.27	28
pañca-ṣāsu tri-yāmāsu	13.28	29
prati-kṣaṇaṁ navya-vad acyutasya yat	13.2	3
prāyo māyāstu me bhartur	13.37	37
purovad ābdaṁ krīḍantaṁ	13.40	41
purovad āsv api hares	13.25	27

S

sādhu pṛṣṭaṁ mahā-bhāgo	13.1	2
sahopaviṣṭā vipine virejuś	13.8	8
sametya gāvo 'dho vatsān	13.31	31
saṁlālitaḥ svācaritaiḥ praharṣayan	13.23	25
śanair athotthāya vimṛjya locane	13.64	77
śanair niḥsīma vavṛdhe	14.26	28
sapady evābhitaḥ paśyan	13.59	70
sarit-pulinam ānīya	13.4	5
sarvaṁ pṛthak tvaṁ nigamāt	13.39	39
sarvaṁ vidhi-kṛtaṁ kṛṣṇaḥ	13.17	18
sarvān ācaṣṭa vaikuṇṭhaṁ	13.38	38
sarve mitho darśayantaḥ	13.10	10
satām ayaṁ sāra-bhṛtāṁ nisargo	13.2	3
satyāḥ ke katare neti	13.43	44
satya-jñānānantānanda-	13.54	60
śigbhis tvagbhir dṛṣadbhiś ca	13.9	9
sneha-snuta-stanya-payaḥ-sudhāsavaṁ	13.22	24
sphuṭat-saro-gandha-hṛtāli-patrika-	13.5	6
spṛṣṭvā catur-mukuṭa-koṭibhir	13.62	75
śrīvatsāṅgada-do-ratna-	13.48	50
śṛṇuṣvāvahito rājann	13.3	4
svakān svakān vatsatarān apāyayan	13.24	26
svakārthānām iva rajaḥ-	13.50	52
sva-mahi-dhvasta-mahibhir	13.53	56
svayaiva māyayājo 'pi	13.44	46
svayam ātmātma-govatsān	13.20	22

T

tad-dhāmnābhūd ajas tūṣṇīṁ	13.56	63
tad-īkṣaṇotprema-rasāplutāśayā	13.33	33
tamyāṁ tamovan naihāraṁ	13.45	48
tān dṛṣṭvā bhaya-santrastān	13.13	13
tan-mātaro veṇu-rava-tvarotthitā	13.22	24
tataḥ kṛṣṇo mudaṁ kartuṁ	13.18	19
tataḥ pravayaso gopās	13.34	34
tathāgha-vadanān mṛtyo	13.4	5
tatheti pāyayitvārbhā	13.7	7
tato nṛponmardana-majja-lepanā-	13.23	25
tato 'rvāk pratilabdhākṣaḥ	13.58	69
tato 'tikutukodvṛtya-	13.56	63
tato vatsān adṛṣṭvaitya	13.16	17
tato vidūrāc carato	13.29	30
tatrodvahat paśupa-vaṁśa-	13.61	73
tat-tad-ātmābhavad rājaṁs	13.21	23
tat-tad-vatsān pṛthaṅ nītvā	13.21	23
tāvad etyātmabhūr ātma-	13.40	41
tāvanta eva tatrābdaṁ	13.42	43
tāvat sarve vatsa-pālāḥ	13.46	49
tiṣṭhan madhye sva-parisuhṛdo	13.11	11

U

ubhāv api vane kṛṣṇo	13.16	17
ubhayāyitam ātmānaṁ	13.18	19
uduhya dorbhiḥ parirabhya mūrdhani	13.33	33
utthāyotthāya kṛṣṇasya	13.63	76

V

vatsāḥ samīpe 'paḥ pītvā	13.6	7
vatsān sakhīn iva purā parito	13.61	73

vatsās tv antar-vane dūraṁ 13.12 12
vicinvan bhagavān kṛṣṇaḥ 13.14 14
vrajasya rāmaḥ premardher 13.35 35

vrajasya sātmanas tokeṣv 13.36 36
vrajaukasāṁ sva-tokeṣu 13.26 28
vṛndāvanaṁ janājīvya- 13.59 70
vyadṛśyanta ghana-śyāmaḥ 13.46 49

Y

yan nūtanayasīśasya 13.1 2
yasya bhāsā sarvam idaṁ 13.55 63
yatra naisarga-durvairāḥ 13.60 71
yāvac chīla-guṇābhidhākṛti-vayo 13.19 20
yāvad vatsapa-vatsakālpaka-vapur 13.19 20
yāvanto gokule bālāḥ 13.41 42

General Index

Numerals in boldface type indicate references to translations of the verses of *Śrīmad-Bhāgavatam.*

A

Abhiṣeka bathing ceremony, Brahmā crying at Kṛṣṇa's feet as, 76
Absolute Truth
  Brahmā saw, **73**
  devotional service reveals, 62
  impersonalist's understanding of, 61
  Kṛṣṇa as, 76
  manifest & unmanifest, 66
  See also: Cause, ultimate; Kṛṣṇa, Lord
Ācāryas (saintly authorities)
  Kṛṣṇa known via, 21
  See also: Paramahaṁsas; Spiritual masters
Ācāryavān puruṣo veda
  quoted, 21
Acintya-bhedābheda philosophy, 21, 41
Acintya defined, 67
Acintyāḥ khalu ye bhāvā
  quoted, 67
Activities
  of Kṛṣṇa. *See:* Kṛṣṇa, pastimes of
  in Kṛṣṇa consciousness, 9
  material vs. spiritual, 69–70
  pious, devotional service preceded by, 9, 52, 70
  See also: Karma
Āditya-varṇaṁ tamasaḥ parastāt
  quoted, 61
Advaitam acyutam anādim ananta-rūpam
  quoted, 21, 40
Advaita-vādīs. *See:* Māyāvādīs
Advancement, spiritual
  hearing of Lord constantly as sign of, 2–3
  See also: Perfection
Affection. *See:* Love
Aghāsura, **5, 16**
Ahaṅkāra itīyaṁ me
  verse quoted, 40
Āhlādinī potency, 67
Aiśvarya defined, 56
Ajā defined, 56
Ajo nityaḥ śāśvato 'yaṁ purāṇo
  quoted, 68
America, author's ocean voyage to, example of, 73
Analogies
  dramatic player & Kṛṣṇa, 18
  fire & Viṣṇu, 62
  flower fructifying & Kṛṣṇa consciousness blossoming, 55
  glowworm's light & inferior's power, **48**
  golden stick & Brahmā bowing down, **75–76**
  government's power & Kṛṣṇa's power, 47
  heat & *viṣṇu-māyā,* 62
  moonlight & Viṣṇus' smiles, **53**
  ocean & Lord's knowledge, 73
  sleep & death, 69
  snow's darkness & inferior's power, **48**
  swan & *paramahaṁsa,* 4
Ānanda-cinmaya-rasa-pratibhāvitābhiḥ
  quoted, 16
Ānanda defined, 61
Ānanda-mātram ajaraṁ purāṇam
  quoted, 61
Anger
  material vs. spiritual, 4
  See also: Envy
Animals
  in Vṛndāvana, 71–72
  See also: Cows; *other specific animals*

Aṇimā-siddhi defined, 56
Ante nārāyaṇa-smṛtiḥ
quoted, 65
Ants, 55
Anxiety. *See:* Fear; Suffering
Apareyam itas tv anyāṁ
verse quoted, 40
Argument
knowledge by, futility of, 67
See also: Philosophy; Speculation, mental
Āroha-panthā defined, 67
Association
with devotees, 59
with material qualities, 57–58
Asthūlam anaṇv ahrasvam adīrgham
quoted, 68
Aupaniṣadaṁ puruṣam
quoted, 61
Author, the (A.C. Bhaktivedanta Swami Prabhupāda), on ship to America, 73
Authorities, spiritual. *See: Ācāryas; Paramahaṁsas;* Spiritual masters
Avaroha-panthā defined, 67–68
Avatāra defined, 67

B

Balarāma (Baladeva), Lord
Brahmā as bewildered on birthday of, 42
Kṛṣṇa above, 57
Kṛṣṇa's expansion pastime revealed to, 29–30, **35–38, 39**–40
lunching with Kṛṣṇa & cowherd boys, 10
quoted on Kṛṣṇa expanding as calves & boys, **39**
yogamāyā amazed, in expansion pastime, 35–37, 42
Bathing
of Baladeva on His birthday, 42
of Kṛṣṇa's feet by Brahmā's tears, **75**–76
Beauty
in Kṛṣṇa consciousness, 9, 55
of Vṛndāvana forest, **6**–7
Bee(s), **6,** 12
Bhagavad-gītā
cited on Kṛṣṇa as Supersoul, 29
materialist dismisses, 73
quoted on association with material qualities, 58, 59
quoted on Kṛṣṇa as seen always, 9
quoted on Kṛṣṇa bewildering the materially born, 17
quoted on matter & spirit, 40
quoted on nature's control, 55
quoted on soul, 68
Bhagavān. *See:* Kṛṣṇa, Lord
Bhaktas. See: Devotees
Bhakta-sane vāsa
quoted, 59
Bhakti. See: Devotional service; Kṛṣṇa, love for, worship of
Bhaktivedanta Swami Prabhupāda, A.C. (the author), on ship to America, 73
Bhaktivinoda Ṭhākura, quoted on men in *māyā*, 69–70
Bhaktyāham ekayā grāhyaḥ
quoted, 61
Bhavāmbudhiḥ defined, 14
Bhavāmbudhir vatsa-padaṁ paraṁ padaṁ
quoted, 13
verse quoted, 14
Bhaya defined, 4
Bhayaṁ dvitīyābhiniveśataḥ syāt
quoted, 13
Bhrama defined, 16
Bhūmir āpo 'nalo vāyuḥ
verse quoted, 40
Bible, the, cited on man in God's image, 76
Birds of Vṛndāvana forest, **6**–7
Birth, four defects follow, 16
Birth-death cycle
Kṛṣṇa consciousness movement vs., 70
See also: Birth; Death
Bliss, transcendental
Brahmā in, **64**
seeing Kṛṣṇa as, 9
See also: Enjoyment; Happiness; Pleasure
Body, material
by-products of, example of, 40

Body, material
demigods award, 55
by modes of nature, 59
See also: Senses
Bondage, material
liberation from, 21
See also: Birth-death cycle; Life, material; *Māyā;* Suffering
Boys, cowherd. *See:* Cowherd boyfriends of Kṛṣṇa
Brahmā, Lord
Absolute Truth seen by, **73**
bewilderment of, on Baladeva's birthday, 42
birth of, 16
in bliss, **64**
calves & boys seen by, in Viṣṇu forms, **49–65,** 66
compared to golden stick, **75–**76
consciousness regained by, **69**
cowherd boys & calves taken by, **16,** 17, 19
cried at Kṛṣṇa's feet, **75–**76, 78
as demigod, 64
entangled in Kṛṣṇa's *māyā,* **16,** 18, 19–20
innumerable, 47
Kṛṣṇa above, 17, 57, 64, 66, 67, 73–74
Kṛṣṇa bewildered, 16–17, 19–20
Kṛṣṇa mystified, as boys & calves, **41–46,** 47, **63–65,** 66–68
Kṛṣṇa questioned by, in Dvārakā, 47, 74
Kṛṣṇa removed *yogamāyā* from, **65,** 66
Kṛṣṇa seen by, as cowherd boy, **73,** 74, 76
Kṛṣṇa's identity realized by, 74, 76, 77
mystic power of, Kṛṣṇa excelled, **43, 44, 46,** 47, 48, 49, 66–68
offered obeisances to Kṛṣṇa, **75,** 76, **77, 78**
quoted on Kṛṣṇa as original Nārāyaṇa, 57
as Sarasvatī's Lord, **65,** 66
time of, vs. earth time, 41–42
Vṛndāvana seen by, **70**
worshiped Viṣṇu, **54**
Brahman (impersonal Absolute)
defined by negation, 68
See also: Māyāvādīs (impersonalists)
Brahman, Supreme
beyond mental speculation, **65,** 67–68
form of, 61
in Nanda Mahārāja's courtyard, 77
universe manifested by, **63**
See also: Absolute Truth; Kṛṣṇa, Lord
Brāhmaṇas (priests & teachers), 58
Brahma-saṁhitā, quoted
on Brahmās & universes, 47
on Kṛṣṇa's forms, 21, 40
on persons in love with Kṛṣṇa, 3
on pure devotee seeing Kṛṣṇa, 9
Brahma-vimohana-līlā, 17, 19
Brahmeti paramātmeti
quoted, 76
Bṛhad-āraṇyaka Upaniṣad, quoted on Brahman, 68

C

Caitanya-caritāmṛta, quoted
on Kṛṣṇa as master of all, 54–55, 57
on opulences of Supreme Lord, 56
on pious births & deaths, repeated, 70
on Rādhā & Kṛṣṇa, 67
Caitanya Mahāprabhu
philosophy of, 41
quoted on materialist vs. spiritualist, 4
Calves
Brahmā saw, in Viṣṇu forms, **49–65,** 66
Brahmā took away, **16,** 17, 19
cows' affection for, **30–32, 35,** 36–37
Kṛṣṇa saved, from Aghāsura, **5**
as Kṛṣṇa's expansions, **19–23, 26, 29,** 29–30, 34, 35, **38, 39–**40, **41,** 42, 43, 44, 51
strayed from Kṛṣṇa & cowherd boys, **12–14**
in Viṣṇu forms, **49–65,** 66
See also: Cows
Catur-bāhu defined, 76
Cause, ultimate
emanations from, 40–41
Kṛṣṇa as, 74, 76

Cause, ultimate (*continued*)
See also: Absolute Truth
Ceta etair anāviddhaṁ
verse quoted, 58
Cid-acit-samanvayaḥ
quoted, 40
Civilization. *See:* Society, human; *Varṇāśrama-dharma*
Conditioned soul
position of, 47
See also: Human being; Living entities; Nondevotees
Cowherd boyfriends of Kṛṣṇa
Brahmā saw, in Viṣṇu forms, **49–65,** 66
Brahmā took away, **16,** 17, 19
Kṛṣṇa assured, about missing calves, **13, 14**
Kṛṣṇa pleased mothers of, as their sons, **24, 25**
Kṛṣṇa saved, from Aghāsura, **5**
as Kṛṣṇa's expansions, 16, **19–23, 29,** 29–30, 34, 37, **38, 39–40, 41,** 42
lunching with Kṛṣṇa, **7–15**
pious past of, 52
three named, 23, 27
in Viṣṇu forms, **49–65,** 66
Cowherd men's affection for sons, **32–34**
Cowherd women (*gopīs*), Kṛṣṇa as "sons" of, 24–25, **27, 28**
Cows
affection of, for calves, **30–32, 35,** 36–37
as Kṛṣṇa's expansions, **26**
sādhus keep, 71
See also: Calves
Cranes of Vṛndāvana forest, 7
Creation, the
elements for, **56**
See also: Material world; Nature, material; Planets; Spiritual world; Universe(s)
Cuckoos of Vṛndāvana forest, 7

D

Daivī hy eṣā guṇamayī
verse quoted, 47
Daṇḍavat defined, 75–76
Danger
in material world, 14
See also: Fear; Suffering
Death
compared to sleep, 69
fear of, 13
as inertia for some time, 69
Kṛṣṇa controls, 13
See also: Birth-death cycle
Defects, the four, 16
Definition by negation, 68
Demigod(s)
body awarded by, 55
Brahmā as, 64
ground never touched by, 76
Kṛṣṇa above, 17, 57, 64
Nārāyaṇa above, 64
See also: Devotees; Heavenly planets' denizens; *specific demigods*
Desire
fulfillment of, 55
of Kṛṣṇa, 57
material vs. spiritual, 53
See also: Kṛṣṇa, love for; Lust; Sense gratification
Devotees of Lord Kṛṣṇa (Vaiṣṇavas)
association with, 59
desire devotional service, 53
as fearless, 13
hearing Lord's pastimes constantly, 2–3
Kṛṣṇa realized by, 74
māyā as seen by, 66
Māyāvādīs vs., 40–41, 66, 68
philosophy of, 40–41
pure devotees desire devotional service, 53
pure devotees see Kṛṣṇa, 9
in Vṛndāvana, 72
worship the Lord, **51,** 52
Devotional service to Lord Kṛṣṇa
Absolute Truth known by, 62
devotees desire, 53
Lord known by, 61, 62
māyā vs., 54
persons in. *See:* Devotees
pious activities precede, 9, 52, 70

Devotional service
purification by, 58
renunciation by, 58–59
in Vṛndāvana, 54, 71, 72
See also: Kṛṣṇa, love for; Kṛṣṇa consciousness
Disciple
submissive, spiritual master enlightens, **5**
See also: Devotees
Dramatic player & Kṛṣṇa, analogy of, 18
Ducks of Vṛndāvana forest, 7
Durban Post report on Kṛṣṇa temple, 72
Duty, Lord free of, 15
Dvārakā, Brahmā & Kṛṣṇa in, 47, 74

E

Earth planet
time on, vs. Brahmā's time, 41–42
See also: Material world
Eating. *See:* Lunch; *Prasāda*
Ecstasy. *See:* Bliss, transcendental; Enjoyment; Happiness; Kṛṣṇa, love for
Ego, false, 56
Ekale īśvara kṛṣṇa, āra saba bhṛtya
quoted, 57
verse quoted, 54, 57
Ekaṁ bahu syām
quoted, 20, 40
Eko nārāyaṇa āsīn na brahmā neśānaḥ
quoted, 64
Elements, material
twenty-four listed, 56
See also: Energy, material; Nature, material
Energies of Kṛṣṇa. *See:* Kṛṣṇa, energies of
Energy, material
birth via, 16
Kṛṣṇa beyond, 17
spiritual energy vs., 35
See also: Elements, material; Material world; *Māyā;* Modes of nature; Nature, material
Enjoyment
of Kṛṣṇa & cowherd boys lunching, **8–12**
Enjoyment
See also: Bliss, transcendental; Happiness; Pleasure
Enlightenment. *See:* Absolute Truth; Knowledge; Kṛṣṇa consciousness
Entanglement, material
items of, 59
See also: Birth-death cycle; Bondage, material
Envy
sense gratification breeds, 71
See also: Anger
Evaṁ paramparā-prāptam
quoted, 68

F

False ego, 56
Fear
of death, 13
devotee free of, 13
of forest, 71–72
Kṛṣṇa controller of, **13**–14
material vs. spiritual, 4
Fire
heat of, example of, 41
Viṣṇu compared to, 62
Flower fructifying & Kṛṣṇa consciousness blossoming, analogy of, 55
Food
distribution of, 72
See also: Lunch, Kṛṣṇa & cowherd boys eating
Forest, Vṛndāvana, **6**–7, 71–72
Form
of God. *See:* Kṛṣṇa, form of; Viṣṇu, forms of
in Kṛṣṇa consciousness, 55
Freedom. *See:* Independence; Liberation
Fruitive activity. *See: Karma;* Sense gratification

G

Glowworm's light & inferior's power, analogy of, **48**

God. *See:* Kṛṣṇa, Lord (Supreme Personality of Godhead)
God consciousness
good qualities by, 72
See also: Kṛṣṇa consciousness
Goddess of fortune, emblem of, Lord possesses, **50**
"Gods." *See:* Demigods
Gokula, **43**
Golden stick & Brahmā bowing down, analogy of, **75–76**
Goodness, mode of (*sattva-guṇa*)
elevation to, 58
Viṣṇus' smiles resembled, **53**
Gopīs (cowherd women), Kṛṣṇa as "sons" of, 24–25, **27, 28**
Govardhana Hill, cows ran from, to calves, **30–32**
Government's power, Kṛṣṇa's power compared to, 47
Govindam ādi-puruṣaṁ tam ahaṁ bhajāmi
quoted, 74
Greed, 58
Guṇas. See: Modes of nature; *specific modes*

H

Haṁsa defined, 4, 7
Happiness
by Kṛṣṇa consciousness, 46–47, 72
trees & vegetables give, 70
in Vṛndāvana, 72
See also: Bliss, transcendental; Enjoyment; Pleasure
Harāv abhaktasya kuto mahad-guṇāḥ
quoted, 72
Hare Kṛṣṇa movement. *See:* Kṛṣṇa consciousness movement
Hari hari viphale janama goṅāinu
quoted, 58, 59
Hearing
Kṛṣṇa's pastimes, 2–3
Śrīmad-Bhāgavatam, 58, 62
Heart, Supersoul in, 29
Heat, *viṣṇu-māyā* compared to, 62
Heat & fire, example of, 41
Heavenly planets' denizens
Kṛṣṇa's lunching with cowherd boys amazed, **11–12**
See also: Demigods
Hlādinī śaktir asmāt
quoted, 17
Human being
Lord resembles, 76
purification for, 58
spiritual life for, 69–70
See also: Conditioned soul; Living entities

I

Identity. *See:* Kṛṣṇa consciousness; Soul; Spirit
Ignorance, mode of (*tamo-guṇa*)
abatement of, 58
See also: Māyā
Imaṁ rājarṣayo viduḥ
quoted, 68
Impersonalists. *See: Jñānīs;* Māyāvādīs
Independence
of Kṛṣṇa, 57
See also: Liberation
Intelligence
of Lord & living entity contrasted, 73
See also: Knowledge
International Society for Krishna Consciousness (ISKCON). *See:* Kṛṣṇa consciousness movement
Īśvaraḥ paramaḥ kṛṣṇaḥ
quoted, 74
Itthaṁ satāṁ brahma-sukhānubhūtyā
verse quoted, 52

J

Janma karma ca me divyam
verse quoted, 21
Janma-koṭi-sukṛtair na labhyate
quoted, 70
Jīva-bhūtāṁ mahā-bāho
verse quoted, 40

Jīva Gosvāmī
cited on God's inconceivability, 67
quoted on Rādhā & Kṛṣṇa, 22
Jīvera 'svarūpa' haya—kṛṣṇera 'nitya-dāsa'
quoted, 54
Jñāna. See: Knowledge
Jñānīs (mental speculators), **60**
See also: Brāhmaṇas; Philosophers

K

Kāla defined, **57**, 59
Kāma defined, 4, **57**, 59
Kāmaṁ kṛṣṇa-karmārpaṇe
quoted, 4
Kāraṇaṁ guṇa-saṅgo 'sya
quoted, 58, 59
Karaṇāpāṭava defined, 16
Karma
defined, **57**, 59
life according to, 69
See also: Activities
Kaustubha gem, Lord possesses, **50**, 51
Kingdom of God. *See:* Spiritual world; Vṛndāvana
Knowledge
descending process of, 67–68
of Kṛṣṇa, 21
Vedic. *See:* Vedic knowledge
See also: Absolute Truth; Intelligence
Kokila defined, 7
Krodha defined, 4
Krodhaṁ bhakta-dveṣi jane
quoted, 4
Kṛṣṇa, Lord (Supreme Personality of Godhead)
abode of. *See:* Vṛndāvana
above all, 17
as Absolute Truth, 76
ācāryas reveal, 21
activities of. *See:* Kṛṣṇa, pastimes of
as Acyuta, 21
Aghāsura killed by, **16**
all-pervading & aloof, 21
arguing with, 67

Kṛṣṇa, Lord
Baladeva under, 57
Balarāma enlightened by, about expansion pastime, 29–30, **35–38**, **39**–40
bewilders the materially born, 16, 17
beyond bewilderment, 46, 47
beyond commands, 56
beyond material energy, 17
boys & calves saved by, from Aghāsura, **5**
Brahmā bewildered by, 16–17, 19–20
Brahmā cried at feet of, **75**–76, 78
& Brahmā in Dvārakā, 47, 74
Brahmā mystified by, as boys & calves, **41–46**, 47, **63–65**, 66–68
Brahmā offered obeisances to, **75**, 76, **77**, **78**
Brahmā put in his place by, 74
Brahmā realized identity of, 74, 76, 77
Brahmā relieved by, from *yogamāyā*, **65**, 66
Brahmā saw, as cowherd boy, **73**, 74, 76
Brahmā under, 17, 57, 64, 66, 67, 73–74
as cause of all, 74, 76
challenge to, futility of, 46–47
compared to dramatic player, 18
complete & changeless, 21
consciousness of. *See:* Kṛṣṇa consciousness
as controller, **13–14**
as cowherd boy, **73**, 74, 76
cowherd boyfriends of. *See:* Cowherd boyfriends
created pleasure for calves' & boys' mothers, **19**–20
as creator, **19**–20
as death's controller, 13
demigods under, 17, 57, 64
desire of, 57
devotees of. *See:* Devotees
devotional service to. *See:* Devotional service
does what He likes, 56
eats sacrificial offerings, **11–12**
energies of
inferior & superior, 40–41
Kṛṣṇa acts by, 15
material & spiritual, 40–41

Kṛṣṇa, Lord (*continued*)
energies of
as one in many, 66–67
See also: Kṛṣṇa, potency of
everything comes from, 21, 63
expansion(s) of
calves as, **19–23, 26, 29,** 29–30, 34 35, **38, 39**–40, **41,** 42, 43, 44, 51
cowherd boys as, 16, **19–23, 29,** 29–30, 34, 37, **38, 39**–40, **41,** 42
cows as, **26**
everything as, 40
Rādhārāṇī as, 22–23
See also: Kṛṣṇa, form of
as fear's controller, **13**–14
food from (*prasāda*), 72
form of
Kṛṣṇa reveals, as He chooses, 60
Māyāvādīs misunderstand, 61
as original person, 21
as transcendental, 61
See also: Kṛṣṇa, expansions of
as *gopīs*' "sons," 24–25, **27, 28**
hearing about, 2–3
in human form, 76
immeasurable, 73
inconceivable, 67
independent, 57
infallible, 21
intelligence of, 73
known by His mercy, 60
known via *ācāryas*, 21
knows everything, 19, 73
liberation by knowing, 21
living entities as servants of, 54–55
lotus feet of, as shelter, 13–14
love for (*bhakti*)
in cowherd boys' mothers, **24, 25–26**
in cowherd men, 33, 34
in elderly *gopīs*, 24–25, **27, 28**
hearing of Lord constantly as sign of, 2–3
purification by, 76

Kṛṣṇa, Lord
love for
in Vrajabhūmi, **28**
See also: Devotional service
lunching with cowherd boys, **7–15**
man in image of, 76
as master of all, 55, 57
mercy of, Lord known by, 60
mercy of, on cowherd boys & calves, 15
mystic power of, Brahmā baffled by, **37, 43, 44, 46,** 47, 48, 49, 66–68
Nārāyaṇa under, 57
as one & different, 21, **39,** 40–41
opulence of, 38, 39, 51, 56, 67
as original person, 21
as Parabrahman, 76
paramahaṁsas devoted to, **3–4**
pastimes of
bewildering Brahmā, 16–17, 19
as confidential & confounding, **5**
hearing of, 2–3
via His energies, 15
as transcendental, 58
via *yogamāyā*, 42
philosophers challenge, 46, 47
potency of
inconceivable, 22–23
invincible, 47
as one & different, 40–41, 66–67
pleasure, 16–17, 23
as supreme, 17
three listed, 67
See also: Kṛṣṇa, energies of; *Māyā; Yogamāyā*
pretended perplexity over missing calves & boys, **18**
pure devotee sees, 9
quoted
on missing calves, His looking for, **13,14**
on *paramparā* system, 68
on Vṛndāvana forest, **6**
See also: Bhagavad-gītā, quoted . . .
Rādhārāṇī as potency of, 22–23, 67
by river with boys & calves, **5–8**

Kṛṣṇa, Lord
  scientists challenge, 46, 47
  seen by pure devotee, 9
  Śiva under, 57, 64
  as Supersoul, 29
  as Supreme Lord, 21, 74, 76
  surrender to, liberation by, 46–47
  temple (ISKCON) of, 7, 52, 53, 72
  topics about, 4
  unconquerable, 46–47
  universe mystified by, 46–47
  Viṣṇu included in, 51
  worship of, **51**, 52, 55, 58
  as *yajña-bhuk*, **11–12**
  as Yaśodā's son, 24
  See also: Absolute Truth; Brahman, Supreme; Nārāyaṇa, Lord; Viṣṇu, Lord
Kṛṣṇa-Balarāma temple, 7, 52, 53
Kṛṣṇa consciousness
  activities in, 9
  appreciation of, 72
  coming to, compared to flower fructifying, 55
  defined, 57
  fear from lack of, 13
  fear of losing, 4
  happiness by, 72
  mentality of, 72
  in one lifetime, 70
  persons in. *See:* Devotees
  in Vṛndāvana, 71, 72
  See also: Devotional service
Kṛṣṇa consciousness movement
  vs. birth-death cycle, 70
  as Kṛṣṇa-centered, 9
  purpose of, 59
Kṛṣṇa-kathā (topics of Kṛṣṇa), 4
Kṛṣṇa-māyā. See: Kṛṣṇa, energies of; *Māyā;* Mystic power; *Yogamāyā*
Kṛṣṇotkīrtana-gāna-nartana-parau
  quoted, 72
Kṛta-puṇya-puñjāḥ
  quoted, 9, 70
Kūjat-kokila-haṁsa-sārasa-gaṇākīrṇe
  quoted, 7

L

Laughter of Kṛṣṇa & cowherd boys lunching, 10, 12
Liberation
  by knowing Kṛṣṇa, 21
  sārūpya-mukti, 50–51
  by surrender to Kṛṣṇa, 46–47
  See also: Independence; Kṛṣṇa consciousness; Purification
Life
  karma determines, 69
  perfection of. *See:* Perfection
  trees & vegetables sustain, 70–71
  in Vṛndāvana, 72
  See also: Animals; Human being; Living entities; Soul; Spirit
Life, material
  as "I live, you die," 72
  person in. *See:* Materialist
  spiritual life contrasted to, 4
  See also: Birth-death cycle; Bondage, material; Entanglement, material; Material world; *Māyā*
Living entities
  everywhere, 74–75
  as individuals, 38
  as Kṛṣṇa's servants, 54–55
  lust & greed entangle, 58
  moving & nonmoving, 55
  worshiped Viṣṇu forms, **54,** 55
  See also: Animals; Human beings; Life; Soul; Soul, conditioned; Spirit
Lotus flower, Brahmā born of, 16
Love
  of cows for calves, **31, 32, 35,** 36–37
  for Kṛṣṇa. *See:* Devotional service; Kṛṣṇa, love for
  material vs. spiritual, 53
Lunch, Kṛṣṇa & cowherd boys eating, **7–15**

Lust, 58
See also: Sense gratification; Sex life

M

Machine's parts, example of, 66–67
Mad-bhaktiṁ labhate parām
quoted, 61
Madhumaṅgala, 12
Magic power. *See:* Mystic power
Mahā-bhāgavata (topmost devotee), 54
See also: Devotees, pure devotees . . .
Mahāmāyā. See: Māyā (Mahāmāyā)
Mahārāja Nanda, prayer to worship, 77
Mahārāja Parīkṣit, **2**, 3
Mahat-tattva, **56**
Mahā-varāha Purāṇa, quoted on Lord's forms, 61
Mahimā-siddhi defined, 56
Mama māyā duratyayā
quoted, 46
Mām eva ye prapadyante
verse quoted, 47
Maṅgala-ārātrika ceremony, 58
Mankind. *See:* Human being; Society, human
Material body. *See:* Body, material
Material energy. *See:* Energy, material
Materialist
attached to women & money, 4
knowledge process of, 67, 68
mentality of, 73
spiritualist contrasted to, 4
See also: Conditioned soul; Māyāvādīs
Material life. *See:* Life, material
Material nature, 55, 56
See also: Energy, material; *Māyā;* Modes of nature
Material world
creation of, **56**
danger in, 14
desire in, 53
fear in, 13–14
forest animals in, 71
four defects in, 16
materialistic mentality of, 73
Material world
passion in, 53
person in. *See:* Materialist
spiritual world vs. 4, 53
Vṛndāvana vs., 71–72
See also: Earth planet; Energy, material; Life, material; *Māyā;* Material nature; Modes of nature; Universe(s)
Mat-sthāni sarva-bhūtāni
quoted, 21
Matter
spirit contrasted to, 40–41
See also: Elements, material; Energy, material; Material nature; Material world
Māyā (Mahāmāyā), 35, 66
Bhaktivinoda Ṭhākura quoted on men in, 69–70
vs. devotional service, 54
implication in & freedom from, 46–47
Māyāvāda vs. Vaiṣṇava view of, 66
See also: Energy, material; False ego; Life, material; Material world; Modes of nature; Mystic power; *Yogamāyā*
Mayādhyakṣeṇa prakṛtiḥ
quoted, 15
Māyāra vaśe, yāccha bhese
quoted, 69
Māyā-śakti. See: Kṛṣṇa, energies of; *Māyā;* Mystic power
Māyāśritānāṁ nara-dārakeṇa
verse quoted, 52
Māyāvādīs (impersonalists)
Lord's form misunderstood by, 61
māyā as seen by, 66
philosophy of, 40–41
quoted on spirit & matter, 40
Vaiṣṇavas vs., 40–41, 66, 68
See also: Jñānīs; Philosophers
Meditation. *See:* Kṛṣṇa consciousness; *Yoga*
Milk
of *gopīs*, Kṛṣṇa drank, 24–25
in swan-*paramahaṁsa* analogy, 4
Vṛndāvana's *sādhus* give, to tigers, 71
Mind, 56

Mind
See also: Intelligence; Kṛṣṇa consciousness
Misery. *See:* Fear; Suffering
Mlecchas, elevation of, 59
Modes of nature, 57–58, 59
See also: Energy, material; *Māyā; specific modes*
Mohitaṁ nābhijānāti
quoted, 17
Mokṣa. See: Liberation
Money, materialist attached to, 4
Monists. *See: Jñānīs;* Māyāvādīs
Monkeys in Vṛndāvana, 72
Moonlight & Viṣṇus' smiles, analogy of, **53**
Mother(s)
of cowherd boys, Kṛṣṇa pleased, **24, 25**
sons loved by, 27
Mother Yaśodā, 24
Muhyanti yat sūrayaḥ
quoted, 17, 64
Mukti. See: Liberation
Muṇḍaka Upaniṣad, quoted on Lord known by His mercy, 60
Mysticism. *See:* Kṛṣṇa consciousness; *Yoga*
Mystic power (*Māyā*)
of Brahmā & Kṛṣṇa contrasted, 16–17, **43, 44, 46,** 47, 48, 49, 66–68
inferior vs. superior, **48**
of Kṛṣṇa, **37**
of Viṣṇu, 56
See also: Māyā (Mahāmāyā); Yogamāyā
Mystics. *See:* Devotees

N

Na cainaṁ kledayanty āpo
verse quoted, 68
Nainaṁ chindanti śastrāṇi
verse quoted, 68
Na jāyate mriyate vā
quoted, 68
Nanda Mahārāja, prayer to worship, 77
Nārāyaṇa, Lord
demigods under, 64
as four-armed, 76
Nārāyaṇa, Lord
Kṛṣṇa above, 57
perfection by remembering, 64–65
See also: Kṛṣṇa, Lord; Viṣṇu, Lord
Nārāyaṇaḥ paro 'vyaktāt
quoted, 64
Nārāyaṇas tvaṁ na hi sarva-dehinām
quoted, 57
Narottama dāsa Ṭhākura, quoted
on association with devotees, 59
of human life's purpose, 58, 59
Naṣṭa-prāyeṣv abhadreṣu
quoted, 58
Na tāṁs tarkeṇa yojayet
quoted, 68
Na tasya kāryaṁ karaṇaṁ ca vidyate
quoted, 15
Nature, material, 55, 56
See also: Energy, material; Material world; *Māyā;* Modes of nature
Nāyam ātmā pravacanena labhyo
verse quoted, 60
Negation, definition by, 68
Neti neti
quoted, 68
Nigama-kalpataror galitaṁ phalam
quoted, 62
Nirvāṇa. See: Bliss, transcendental; Liberation
Nityaṁ nava-navāyamānam
quoted, 2
Nondevotees
anger against, 4
See also: Jñānīs; Materialist; Māyāvādīs; Philosophers

O

Obeisances (*daṇḍavat*), 75–76
Ocean, Lord's knowledge compared to, 73
Opulences
of Kṛṣṇa, 38, 39, 51, 67
of Viṣṇu, 56
See also: Money; Mystic power; Power

P

Padaṁ padaṁ yad vipadām
quoted, 14
Padyāvali, quoted on worshiping Nanda Mahārāja, 77
Paramahaṁsas (topmost transcendentalists), **3–4**
See also: Devotees, pure devotees . . .
Paramparā system, 68
Parāsya śaktir vividhaiva śrūyate
quoted, 15, 66, 67
Parīkṣit Mahārāja, **2,** 3
Passion, mode of (*rajo-guṇa*)
abatement of, 58
Viṣṇus' glance resembled, **53**
Pastimes of Kṛṣṇa. *See:* Kṛṣṇa, pastimes of
Paśyanty ātmani cātmānam
verse quoted, 62
Peacocks of Vṛndāvana forest, 7
Perfection(s)
by remembering Nārāyaṇa, 64–65
seeing Kṛṣṇa as, 9
via spiritual life, 69–70
of *yoga,* 56
Personalists. *See:* Devotees
Philosophers
Kṛṣṇa challenged by, 46, 47
See also: Ācāryas; Jñānīs; Māyāvādīs; Spiritual masters
Philosophy
acintya-bhedābheda, 21, 41
Māyāvāda vs. Vaiṣṇava, 40–41
See also: Absolute Truth; Knowledge
Pilgrimage place, Vṛndāvana temple as, 53
Pious activities, devotional service preceded by, 9, 52, 70
Planets
scientist's consideration of, 74–75
See also: Creation, the; Earth planet; Stars; Sun; Universe(s)
Pleasure
Kṛṣṇa expands for, 16–17, 23
See also: Bliss, transcendental; Enjoyment; Happiness; Sense gratification
Power
inferior vs. superior, **48**
of Kṛṣṇa. *See:* Kṛṣṇa, potency of
See also: Mystic power; Opulences
Prakṛteḥ kriyamāṇāni
quoted, 55
Pramāda defined, 16
Prasāda in Vṛndāvana, 72
Premāñjana-cchurita-bhakti-vilocanena
quoted, 61
verse quoted, 3
Pure devotees. *See:* Devotees, pure devotees . . .
Purification
by *bhakti,* 76
by devotional service, 58
human life for, 58
via Vedic knowledge, 61
See also: Liberation
Pūrṇasya pūrṇam ādāya
quoted, 21
Pūtanā, 58

Q

Qualities, material, 57–58, 59
See also: Energy, material; *Māyā*

R

Rādhā-kṛṣṇa-bhajana defined, 58
Rādhā kṛṣṇa-praṇaya-vikṛtir
quoted, 22, 67
Rādhā-Kṛṣṇa worship, 58
Rādhārāṇī as Kṛṣṇa's pleasure potency, 22–23, 67
Rajo-guṇa. See: Passion, mode of
Rāvaṇa, *māyā* Sītā taken by, 17
Reality. *See:* Absolute Truth; Kṛṣṇa consciousness; Spiritual world
Reflection of sun in waterpots, example of, 62
Religion. *See:* Devotional service; Kṛṣṇa, surrender to, liberation by; Kṛṣṇa consciousness; Purification

Renunciation by devotional service, 58–59
Rice, Kṛṣṇa holding, **11, 14**
River, Kṛṣṇa, boys, & calves by, **5–8**

S

Ṣaḍ-aiśvaryaiḥ pūrṇo ya iha bhagavān
quoted, 56
Sādhus (saintly persons)
in Vṛndāvana, 71
See also: Ācāryas; Devotees; *Paramahaṁsas;* Spiritual masters
Śakti. See: Kṛṣṇa, energies of
Śakti-śaktimator abhedaḥ
quoted, 40
Salvation. *See:* Liberation
Samagra-jagat viṣṇumayam
quoted, **21**
Samāśritā ye pada-pallava-plavaṁ
verse quoted, 14
Samatvenaiva vīkṣeta
verse quoted, 57, 64
Saṁskāra defined, **57,** 59
Saṁvit potency, 67
Sanātana Gosvāmī, cited on Lord creating devotee's desire to serve Him, 53
Sandarśanaṁ viṣayinām atha yoṣitāṁ ca
quoted, 4
Sandhinī potency, 67
Śaṅkarācārya, quoted on Nārāyaṇa's supremacy, 64
Santaḥ sadaiva hṛdayeṣu vilokayanti
quoted, 4, 9
Śāntika-snāna ceremony, 42
Sārasa defined, 7
Sarasvatī, goddess, **65,** 66
Sārūpya-mukti defined, 50–51
Sarva-dharmān parityajya
quoted, 46
Sarva-kāma-dughā mahī
quoted, 71
Sarvaṁ khalv idaṁ brahma
quoted, 21
Sarvaṁ viṣṇumayaṁ jagat
quoted, 21
Sarvataḥ pāṇi-pādam tat
quoted, 9
Sarve nityāḥ śāśvatāś ca
quoted, 61
Sarvopādhi-vinirmuktam
quoted, 76
Śāstras (Vedic scriptures). *See:* Vedic knowledge; Vedic literature; *specific scriptures*
Satellite orbiting earth, example of, 42
Sattva-guṇa. See: Goodness, mode of
Satyaṁ brahma ānanda-rūpam
quoted, 61
Scientists, material
Kṛṣṇa challenged by, 46, 47
planets as considered by, 74–75
Seasons, all, Vṛndāvana's trees in, **70**
Self. *See:* Living entities; Soul; Spirit
Self-realization. *See:* Devotional service; Kṛṣṇa consciousness
Sense gratification
envy due to, 71
See also: Lust; Sex life
Senses
as Creation elements, 56
See also: Body, material; Mind
Service
everyone engaged in, 54–55
See also: Devotional service
Sex life
materialist attached to, **4**
See also: Lust; Sense gratification
Ship in ocean, example of, 73
Sītā, Rāvaṇa took *māyā* form of, 17
Śiva, Lord, Kṛṣṇa above, 57, 64
Sleep, death compared to, 69
Snow's darkness & inferior's power, analogy of, **48**
Society, human
elevation of, 59
God-conscious opportunity for, 72
See also: Human being; *Varṇāśrama-dharma*
Sons, mother's affection for, 27
Soul
defined by negation, 68

Soul (*continued*)
See also: Life; Living entities; Spirit
Soul, conditioned
position of, 47
See also: Human being; Living entities; Nondevotees
Source, ultimate
emanations from, 40–41
Kṛṣṇa as, 74, 76
See also: Absolute Truth
South Africa, Durban, Kṛṣṇa temple in, 72
Speculation, mental
Supreme Brahman beyond, **65**, 67–68
See also: Knowledge; Philosophy
Spirit
matter contrasted to, 40–41
See also: Life; Soul; Spiritual world
Spiritualist, 4
See also: Devotees
Spiritual life
advancement in, 2–3
human life for, 69–70
material life vs., 4
See also: Devotional service; Kṛṣṇa consciousness
Spiritual masters, **5**
See also: Ācāryas; Devotees, pure devotees . . . ; *Paramahaṁsas*
Spiritual world (Vaikuṇṭha), 4, 50–51, 53
See also: Vṛndāvana
Śravaṇaṁ kīrtanaṁ viṣṇoḥ
quoted, 52
Śreyaḥ-kairava-candrikā-vitaraṇam
quoted, 53
Śrīdāmā, 23, 27
Śrīmad-Bhāgavatam
cited on living entities everywhere, 74–75
hearing & discussing, 58, 62
quoted on Absolute Truth known by devotional service, 62
quoted on Brahmā under Kṛṣṇa, 17
quoted on cowherd boys' pious past, 52
quoted on devotee as free from fearful world, 14
quoted on fear, 13
Śrīmad-Bhāgavatam
quoted on hearing *Śrīmad-Bhāgavatam,* 58
quoted on Kṛṣṇa as original Nārāyaṇa, 57
quoted on life's necessities provided by nature, 71
quoted on Lord known by devotional service, 61
quoted on passion & ignorance producing lust & greed, 58
quoted on purification by devotional service, 58
quoted on renunciation by devotional service, 58–59
Śrīvatsa mark, Lord possesses, 51
Śrutim apare smṛtim itare
quoted, 77
Stars
influence of, 55
See also: Earth planet; Creation, the; Planets; Sun; Universe(s)
Subala, 23, 27
Sudāmā, 10, 23, 27
Suffering
by opposing Kṛṣṇa, 46–47
See also: Birth-death cycle; Bondage, material; Fear
Śukadeva Gosvāmī, quoted
on cowherd boys' pious past, 52
on Parīkṣit hearing Lord's pastimes, **2**
Sun
reflection of, in waterpots, example of, 62
See also: Creation, the; Planets; Stars; Universe(s)
Supersoul, 29
Supreme Lord. *See:* Kṛṣṇa, Lord (Supreme Personality of Godhead)
Svabhāva defined, **57**, 59
Svarūpa Dāmodara Gosvāmī, quoted on Rādhā & Kṛṣṇa, 67
Svarūpa-śakti. See: Kṛṣṇa, energies of
Śvetāśvatara Upaniṣad, quoted
on Kṛṣṇa's energy as one in many, 66
on Lord having no duty, 15
on Supreme Person, 61
Swan, *paramahaṁsa* compared to, 4

T

Tac chraddadhānā munayo
 verse quoted, 62
Tadā rajas-tamo-bhāvāḥ
 quoted, 58
 verse quoted, 58
Tamāla tree in Kṛṣṇa-Balarāma temple, 52
Tamo-guṇa (ignorance mode), abatement of, 58
Tears of Brahmā at Kṛṣṇa's feet, **75–76**, 78
Temple, Hare Kṛṣṇa
 in Durban, South Africa, 72
 in Vṛndāvana, 7, 52, 53
Tene brahma hṛdā ya ādi-kavaye
 quoted, 17
Tigers in Vṛndāvana, 71, 72
Time on Earth vs. Brahmā's time, 41–42
Topics of Kṛṣṇa, 4
Transcendence. *See:* Kṛṣṇa consciousness; Liberation; Spiritual world
Transcendentalists. *See: Ācāryas;* Devotees; *Jñānīs; Paramahaṁsas;* Spiritual masters
Tree(s)
 livelihood provided by, **70**–71
 as nonmoving, 55
 tamāla, in Kṛṣṇa-Balarāma temple, 52
 variety in, example of, 66
 in Vṛndāvana, 70
Truth. *See:* Absolute Truth
Tyaktvā dehaṁ punar janma
 verse quoted, 21

U

Universe(s)
 innumerable, 47
 Kṛṣṇa mystifies, 46–47
 living entities everywhere in, 74–75
 Supreme Brahman manifests, **63**
 See also: Creation, the; Earth planet; Nature, material; Planets; Spiritual world; Stars; Sun
Upaniṣads, followers of, 61

V

Vaikuṇṭha. *See:* Spiritual world
Vaiṣṇavas. *See:* Devotees
Vaiṣṇava-toṣaṇī, cited on Śrīvatsa mark, 51
Vana defined, 71
Variety, unity in, 67
Varṇāśrama-dharma, 58
Vāsudeve bhagavati
 quoted, 58
Vedeṣu durlabham adurlabham ātma-bhaktau
 quoted, 74
Vedic knowledge
 acceptance of, 67–68
 purification via, 61
 See also: Absolute Truth; Knowledge
Vedic literature
 Śrīmad-Bhāgavatam as essence of, 62
 See also: specific literatures
Vegetables, **70**–71
Vipralipsā defined, 16
Vīrarāghava Ācārya, cited on material entanglement, 59
Viṣṇu, Lord
 all-pervading, 47
 calves & boys in form of, **49–65**, 66
 compared to fire, 62
 forms of, characteristics & dress of, **49, 50, 51, 53, 60,** 61, 62
 forms of, worship of, **51**, 52, **54**, 55
 Kṛṣṇa includes, 51
 mystic powers of, 56
 qualifications of, 62
 See also: Kṛṣṇa, Lord; Nārāyaṇa, Lord; Supersoul
Viṣṇu-tattva, Kṛṣṇa's calves, cows & boys as, 44
Viśvanātha Cakravartī Ṭhākura, cited
 on Brahmā wiping his eyes, 78
 on Kṛṣṇa removing *yogamāyā* from Brahmā, 66
 on Supreme Brahman, 61
Vraja(bhūmi). *See:* Vṛndāvana

Vṛndāvana (Vraja)
animals in, 71–72
Brahmā saw, **70**
devotees in, 72
devotional service in, 54
forest of, **6**–7, 71–72
happiness in, 72
Kṛṣṇa-Balarāma temple in, 7, 52, 53
Kṛṣṇa consciousness in, 71, 72
Kṛṣṇa entered, after expanding as boys & calves, **22,** 23
as Kṛṣṇa's abode, **71**–72
love for Kṛṣṇa in, **28**
material world vs., 71–72
residents of, *yogamāyā* influenced, during expansion pastime, 35–37
trees in, 70
See also: Spiritual world
Vyāsadeva, *Śrīmad-Bhāgavatam* by, 62

W

Water in swan-*paramahaṁsa* analogy, 4
Waterpots, sun's reflection in, example of, 62
Wisdom. *See:* Absolute Truth; Knowledge; Philosophy
Women
materialist attached to, **4**
See also: Gopīs
Work. *See:* Activities; *Karma*
World. *See:* Earth planet; Material world
Worship. *See:* Devotional service; Kṛṣṇa, worship of; Viṣṇu, forms of, worship of

Y

Yam evaiṣa vṛṇute tena labhyas
verse quoted, 60
Yaṁ śyāmasundaram acintya-
verse quoted, 3
Yāre yaiche nācāya, se taiche kare nṛtya
verse quoted, 54, 57
Yaśodā, Kṛṣṇa son of, 24
Yas tu nārāyaṇaṁ devaṁ
verse quoted, 57, 64
Yasyaika-niśvasita-kālam athāvalambya
quoted, 47
Yavanas, elevation of, 59
Yoga
perfections of, 56
See also: Devotional service; Kṛṣṇa consciousness; Mystic power
Yogamāyā potency
defined, 66
Kṛṣṇa enjoyed via, 23, 25
Kṛṣṇa relieved Brahmā from, **65,** 66
Kṛṣṇa's expansion pastime via, 35–37, 42
See also: Mystic power
Yoga-siddhis defined, 56
Yogīs. See: Devotees
Yogurt, Kṛṣṇa holding, **11, 14**